D1591115

Black Power and the American Myth

BLACK POWER
AND THE
AMERICAN MYTH

C. T. VIVIAN

FORTRESS PRESS   PHILADELPHIA

PRESS

Library of Congress Catalog Card Number 76-101424

2623L69   *Printed in U.S.A.*   *1-1236*

To my wife

who has persevered and has continued to love
and care throughout the years of my being
away from home for the sake of the struggle,

who has continued to rear our children
and transfer to them even in the presence
of radical evil the faith that we both hold
in God and man

CONTENTS

Part I

BACKGROUND TO STRUGGLE

1

The Moral Confrontation

The United States began with a struggle for civil rights. The specific issue—taxation without representation—was merely a focus for the larger question of whether or not a dominant majority would continue to exploit a subject minority. The American colonists decided that this oppression was not tolerable. They began to protest: first by petition, then by demonstration, and when these proved futile, by armed revolt. America was born as a revolutionary nation.

This is the American heritage: the struggle for freedom, the striving to build a land with liberty and justice for . . .

That sentence must remain incomplete. Freedom, liberty, equality, and justice are truly parts of our democratic inheritance; but this is an inheritance which we have never fully claimed, for it is inextricably bound to another—the legacy of slavery. This too is a part of America's tradition; and we have been unable to separate one from the other. We have been unable to make the best of our heritage function because we have been unwilling to rid ourselves of the worst. Slavery remains today an unconquered devil, battling with freedom in the minds and the streets of America. That battle is America's record and its fate.

Fifteen years ago, a new chapter in this record opened, a spontaneous modern response to the condition of the Black minority.* It began with a new kind of confrontation, a new style of leadership, and a new sense of urgency which have since then generated conflicts in many other areas of the national life. It was the beginning of what we now call The Movement.

The nature of this movement is often misunderstood. It has been closely identified with individual leaders. Yet it was not something that leaders did to their people as much as something that people did to make leaders. It included many established interests and sources of power. Yet it was never effectively a coalition established at conference tables. Because it was a national movement it sometimes seemed to be nationally organized. Many of us, in fact, tried to make it operate through national organization. Yet it remained a confluence of local and immediate clashes, a self-sustaining chain reaction to the American experience of Black people throughout the land.

The Movement began as an irrepressible social force generated at the very roots of American society, a movement of people determined to force their nation to accept what that nation claimed were its fundamental values.

Rosa Parks, a seamstress from Montgomery, Alabama, is often given credit for initiating what grew into The Movement. For no reason that has ever been satisfac-

---

*I have carefully considered the use of upper-case and lower-case letters for the terms "Black" and "white." I use "Black" as a self-designation which parallels the white self-designation "Caucasian." On the other hand, the word "white" stands alongside the white man's choice of the word "colored."

torily explained, Rosa Parks on her way home from work one evening sat down in the front of the bus and refused to move to the back. For this crime she was arrested, and her arrest sparked the Montgomery bus boycott. This boycott brought Dr. Martin Luther King, Jr., into leadership and national prominence. Rosa Parks' sit-in took place on December 5, 1955. Thirteen months later, the boycott ended with the integration of the buses.

If we think back to that time, we can remember that Black and white relations had almost always been placed in an economic context. This tradition began with the practical economics of slavery and continued with the theoretical economics of freedom. The question always before the Black man was: What must I do to be free? And the answer that was almost always given by Black and white alike was: Get jobs, salaries, a financial base from which to operate in a materialistic society.

Freedom was conceived of in commercial terms, and indeed there was cause for this. The most visible, and many of the most hideous, aspects of the Black condition were those engendered by poverty. Yet the fact is that when ordinary Black people began to move it was not an economic force which moved them. They sought dignity, not dollars; manhood, not money; pride, not prosperity.

In reviewing the effects of The Movement, this fact is basic to our understanding. It was Martin Luther King who removed the Black struggle from the economic realm and placed it in a moral and spiritual context. It was on this plane that The Movement first confronted

5

the conscience of the nation. This point is crucial, for previously even most Black leaders had been unable to deal with race relations as a moral problem. This was perhaps because the immorality was so immense that it defied ordinary moral categories.

As a nation, America had steadfastly refused to accept the humanity of its Black minority. It had perpetuated an endless series of horrors more ghastly than most of its citizens could imagine or believe.

The excuses contrived throughout the country's history to explain this behavior offer the most fantastic and laborious distortions of fact and experience. Racism began as rationalization. It began as a justification of the white man's injustice to the Black. The greed that brought Black men into slavery was not alone enough to make the institution bearable to the white conscience. Spurious anthropology was created. Heretical theology was contrived. History was rewritten. Law was remade to fit new customs. These constructs provided the framework for viewing Blacks as something less than human.

In their daily lives, white Americans had to become racists or John Browns in order to preserve their mental balance. For if Blacks were not subhuman then an unspeakable and intolerable crime was being committed. Americans generally preferred to believe that there was no crime. Yet there were many more whites of John Brown's persuasion than is commonly known. Sixteen others rode to Harper's Ferry with him. The annals of Southern history document the executions of scores of whites accused of fomenting Black revolt. And the problems which outraged these people are still with us.

6

Today, the Black condition is relatively unchanged. And in relation to the lavish affluence of the total society, the Black condition has clearly worsened. Because of this, bigotry has remained a psychological necessity for white America, bigotry or John Brownism— which is precisely what The Movement has released in so many thousands of the nation's young.

But today bigotry most often shows itself as blind indifference and willful ignorance rather than as racist activism. American society has become schizophrenic, wavering between its twin personalities of democracy and slavery, gripped by social and moral pathology, trapped in "the American dilemma." From the slave quarters of the Old South to the Northern ghettos, white America has developed massive institutions, pervasive social lies, and thoroughgoing mental blocks to prevent itself from seeing Blacks in moral terms, that is, as human beings.

The Movement sought to storm these citadels of blindness so that America would be forced to see. But before sight could be brought to white America, Blacks had to regain their own vision. The blind could not lead the blind. And after four hundred years of systematic negation and active destruction of their humanity, most Blacks saw themselves largely through the crippled eyes of whites.

Economically, it had become impossible for Blacks to enter the society, or even to make themselves visible as men. They were forced to failure and their failure was used as proof against their worth. This had gone on for so long that they, like the whites, often accepted this failure as inevitable if not just.

7

But through The Movement, especially through the searing moral vision of Martin Luther King, Black people in enormous numbers began to accept the moral imperatives of their condition, began to accept themselves as men and women. They saw that justice demanded their release from the economic prison in which they were held. But they saw also that justice must be rooted in the bedrock of humanity. They saw that the moral and spiritual issues were prior, in fact prerequisite.

When Martin Luther King emerged, he raised the issues from the pragmatic to the sublime. In so doing, he heightened the consciousness of the entire country—freeing some from the sickness of hate and exposing the disease in others, allowing some to move to heal themselves and forcing the rest to declare themselves incurable.

This was a spiritual declaration of independence for Blacks and many whites as well, a declaration that rattled the entire nation by destroying much of America's contrived vision of itself. For man sees himself in relation to others, defines himself in terms of his relationships. And it was not just in Alabama and Mississippi that men stood gaping in disorientation, wondering what had happened to the happy Sambo. This occurred across the nation and around the world. And it was just as shocking to Blacks, though generally more joyous, when they were forced to reexamine and redefine themselves.

When this redefinition began, the forward motion of The Movement redoubled. Blacks, having begun to see themselves clearly, marched out to make themselves visible to the rest of society. And, predictably, the society tried to defend itself from the sight. When Blacks marched into the dogs and clubs crying "freedom," the nation reacted by calling them impatient hoodlums, hooligans, and troublemakers with no conception of law and no respect for order. But these hypocrisies were seen all too clearly by those in the teeth of the dogs of law and under the clubs of order.

Men of goodwill were shocked. They pointed to the imaginary accomplishments of tokenism. They heralded the fictional success of patience. They decried the violence. They were still blind to the massive violence which had been heaped upon generations of Blacks. They still protected themselves from the fundamental facts of their nation's existence.

Yet their confusion betrayed them, for they put the protest march in the same category with lynching, and said both were wrong, blaming whites for one and Blacks for the other. Yet Blacks were clearly the victims in both cases. They were no more guilty of creating violence by marching than an assaulted woman is guilty of rape.

The same argument had been brought out during the time of slavery. Abolitionists were accused of violence for merely *advocating* an end to slavery, while the steady falling of the overseer's lash went unquestioned as a necessary fact of life. Now, in the same way, white America has accepted the brutality of enforced poverty, the violence of economic and social discrimination, the viciousness of personal intolerance, as social

9

facts. But hymn singing on a public street, prayer meetings in a courthouse square—these were acts of raw violence, intolerable breaches of the peace. These called for the hounds and the troops, and for scathing denunciation by right-thinking Americans everywhere.

Yet there was a crack, a tiny crevice opened in the national blindness. The wanton cruelty of Southern justice was not entirely absent from the newsphotos of cracking skulls. The hysterical insanity that underlay the national conscience could not be entirely erased from the television reports which showed mobs gathered in trembling rage to shriek and spit between drawn bayonets at an eight-year-old girl who dared to breach the sacred Southern way of life by attending a decent school. America began to see, though it would still not believe.

Part II

FREEDOM ROAD

2

Strategic Goals

During those early years when we were first trying to plan strategy for The Movement, there were five goals that we believed were necessary—five tasks to be accomplished before Freedom could become Now.

We saw that both the Black and the white communities must be changed. We saw that the entire national purpose would have to be refocused. And we saw that in order to actually accomplish these things we would have to find a new method, a method which would fully and finally bring about our success.

At every step we were aware of these goals and we continually weighed one against another as we moved, for we knew that all were necessary and that none could be completely achieved without the others.

3

The Out Class

We saw that the first goal of our movement had to be the creation of a new condition within the Black community, and within Blacks themselves. Merely by examining ourselves and our people, we could see the legacy of slavery and the failure of Reconstruction. We could see the cumulative results of the history which had been forced upon us.

The Blacks who were brought to this country as slaves were systematically stripped of all cultural ties. Care was taken on most plantations to separate slaves who spoke the same language. Only English, a tongue foreign to them all, was permitted. African religions were forbidden. African customs and social organizations were impossible. All vestiges of African society were eradicated. The slaves were stripped of everything that had formerly sustained and defined them—from homeland to friends and family. In fact, every possibility for them to define themselves was removed; only by accident and in unimportant ways could they do so.

Nor were they allowed to develop new institutions to replace the old. They were not permitted to learn to read or write. They were not permitted to meet or talk together in groups except in the presence of white men.

At first, they were not even allowed Christianity—until it was found to be a useful tool for teaching meekness and docility.

Every form of social life which could ordinarily be considered normal was forbidden. Even families in the ordinary sense were impossible. Women were used like cows, as breeders, to replenish and increase the stock. Children were separated from their mothers and sold. Men, even when they were allowed to "marry," had no way of protecting their wives or daughters from the casual lust of white masters and overseers. In fact, Black men were only allowed to perform the procreative act with those women whom the white men didn't want themselves. It was a time when mothers strangled their newborn infants so that they would not have to grow up as slaves.

Blacks were permitted nothing by which to mark themselves as human. They had neither legal nor moral rights. Legally, they were defined as a kind of humanoid cattle. They were property, not people. They had no moral rights for the same reason—they were considered less than human. The closest they came to human status was when each was counted as three-fifths of a man in the census that determined how many representatives a state should have in Congress.

Yet in many ways Blacks were safer while they were still slaves than they were later when they became free men. As slaves they *were* property; they had value. They were branded, beaten, and lashed in the fields. They were whipped on the slightest pretext, tortured for sport, and murdered as examples. Still, a slaveowner usually did not destroy his Black labor any more than a modern farmer would beat his tractor to pieces. But once they were emancipated, this restraint vanished. The value of the Blacks was erased. Four billion dollars worth of property was eliminated by the Thirteenth Amendment. And from that day forth, Blacks could be starved, lynched, or chain-ganged to death without hesitation or consideration.

Even though he was free, the Black man could still not protect his family, either physically or economically. He still had no real rights, although the Constitution had been amended to declare him a citizen. He was neither considered to be, nor treated as, a man.

Yet eventually Blacks began to develop a few social institutions. From the secret "hush harbor" meetings where slaves held church services in their own fashion with a preacher of their own choice, the "invisible institution" of Black Christianity developed. This was the first and most effective institution of the burgeoning culture. From it, other organizations and institutions grew—lodges, schools, burial and ladies' aid societies.

Yet the culture that was formed was deficient. It was modeled on, and colored by, the presuppositions of white culture. Even the Black church, which has been the closest thing in most communities to a truly independent Black institution, has largely failed to deal with the facts of Black America.

The church has taught that Blacks were human, but that they would only enjoy the privileges of that humanity after death, in the sweet bye-and-bye of the Great Beyond. In confining itself to such otherworldly teachings, the church has continued to fulfill the role that white slavemasters set for it. It has kept Blacks submissive, passively accepting their temporal fate, with their eyes and their expectations firmly fixed on the eternal.

As we began planning strategy we could see that the remnants of slave psychology would have to be discarded. Blacks had to come to see themselves as masters of their own fate, masters of their secular destiny as well as their spiritual destiny. So, many of the tactics we chose were directed toward bringing about the kinds of understanding that could lead to this redefinition.

We had all had painful experiences such as seeing a small Black girl, asked to draw her own picture, produce a blonde and blue-eyed portrait. This kind of psychological warping continues into adulthood as a preoccupation with hair straighteners and skin bleaches. This is the ghetto of fantasy in which so many of our people have been trapped.

But there were physical ghettos, too, where Black people were suffering under a multitude of oppressive forces which our strategies would have to overcome. Discrimination occurred in so many forms and with such manifold results that it was virtually impossible to detail.

Economic discrimination created poverty. Poverty and segregated housing combined to form ghetto slums. In these areas, overcrowding and a severe lack of space for recreation left nowhere but the streets for children to play. Thus, in Harlem, for example, children are still killed by automobiles at a rate one-third higher than in the rest of New York City. This is one tiny aspect of the Black condition. If you are trapped in Black Harlem, one-third more of your children die under the wheels of cars.

Another pertinent statistic is the infant mortality rate among Blacks. This is one of the most important indices of community health; and the figures show that the infant mortality rate for Blacks is about twice as high as it is for whites. The maternity death rate is three times as high.

Malnutrition, lack of health-care facilities, neighborhoods forgotten by city services such as garbage collection, and the inability to afford medical attention—all these combine to produce the grim results. If you are Black your babies die twice as often as white babies; and you die three times as often having them.

Nearly half of the Black people in the United States are living below the poverty level established by the Social Security Administration. And it should be remembered that most of the poor in America are in families where someone is working full-time.

It is often pointed out that between 1940 and 1960 the overall income of Black families rose significantly. It is seldom pointed out that the *real* income, the buying power, dropped—inflation ate up every gain that was made. In addition, the discrepancy between white and Black income levels increased during that period. So Blacks fell even further behind the national averages. In Chicago, the average income for Black and white families alike is $7,100. The difference, however, is plain. The figure is true of Black families with two people working and of white families with one person working.

18

These facts—and all of the others which describe the Black condition—we knew well before we began. Our problem was to make the rest of the nation understand them. We knew that these facts were the results of systematic persecution and willful neglect. Our problem was to stop the one and to change the other.

But we did not begin to form our strategy in a vacuum. There were models of social action from the past which had at one time or another begun to create the changes we saw were required. Most of these models had been destroyed in their organizational forms. But their meaning remained, for each of them had provided the systematically deprived Black population with a sense of hope and some power to move.

There were the self-help and industrial education doctrines of Booker T. Washington; the higher education movement and plans for cooperative action of W. E. B. DuBois; the call for racial pride and separatism by Marcus Garvey. And behind all of these were the unforgettable ghosts of Gabriel Prosser, Denmark Vessy, and Nat Turner—all of whom had organized slave revolts. There was also the gigantic figure of Toussaint L'Overture, the Black military and political genius who turned a Haitian riot into a genuine revolution and brought the second republic of the Western Hemisphere into being in 1803.

Among other models of social action was the American Revolution itself. And there was Mahatma Gandhi and the Indian Revolution which yielded a theory of nonviolent force. There was the American labor movement with its action through sit-ins and strikes.

Asa Phillip Randolph, the Black labor organizer, was a bridge between the labor and civil rights movements. He was one of the early advocates of nonviolent demonstrations in support of Black freedom. At the beginning of the Second World War, Randolph forced President Roosevelt to issue Executive Order 8802 which banned discrimination in defense industries and apprenticeship programs. He accomplished this by threatening to bring one hundred thousand Blacks to march on Washington with the demand. Later, during the war, Randolph was instrumental in forcing President Truman to issue the executive order that banned segregation in the Army. Randolph did this by threatening a campaign of massive civil disobedience against the draft.

There were also many models of individual action, men such as the Rev. Charles Lee of Belzoni, Mississippi, who was shot to death for voting, but who kept a heroic tradition alive.

And there was a Black population suddenly intent upon making their expectations a reality, a Black population already moving toward redemption and fulfillment, not only for themselves, but also for the nation. There was a Black population which still believed in America long after it seemed that America had ceased to believe in itself. With these traditions, and this force, we began.

4

The Intercaste

Our second goal was to bring the Black middle class into our struggle. They had the resources which were needed to help The Movement operate. They had money, of course; but, more important, they had talents and technical skills, as lawyers, doctors, architects, business managers, administrators, and churchmen—skills which would be required to change the entire Black community. Blacks form a separate caste in American society. And since there has been virtually no possibility for them to escape from this caste all striving, climbing, and competition for the few available symbols of power and prestige have gone on within the caste. Because of this, classes within the caste have been formed; and even the Black middle class has several more or less distinct branches.

First of all, there are those who have struggled and succeeded, those who have attained prestige through occupational status or wealth—however that wealth was attained. Yet even at their best most of these people have been forced to take their advantages from the fact that there *was* a race problem. Some have been allowed to speak for their people, even to protest along formally acceptable lines, but always as Blacks, not as ordinary men and women.

Thus, the Black social scientist studies the Black condition, not the general condition of society. The Black historian studies Black history, not the history of the nation. This, of course, partly because these studies are needed by Black people. But this is also what is expected of a Black. It is what is allowed.

A second part of the Black middle class is made up of those who have failed to achieve wealth or occupational status, but who nonetheless choose to live as though they had succeeded. It is still a simple fact that a Black college graduate earns about the same amount in his lifetime as a white who has not gone past the eighth grade. This is one of the results of economic discrimination.

So it is still not uncommon for a Black man and his wife, even with some education, to be working at two menial jobs each in order to purchase the trappings of the middle class life to which they aspire. These people form a large proportion of the Black middle class, a segment which is middle class by wishful self-definition.

And, finally, there is a third group in the Black middle class, a group which in many places overlaps the other two. This group has been defined by whites, on the basis of color. Lighter-skinned Negroes have historically been awarded positions of leadership and influence—either directly or indirectly because they received superior educational opportunities.

The special attention paid by whites to these Browns and Tans was not simply because they looked more white, but often because they were directly related. A quick look at the varieties of color among the "Black" population should convince anyone of the extent of miscegenation that has occurred in America. This has been obvious since the earliest days of slavery. A traveler in the early South was told by a planter: "There's not a likely-looking Black girl in the state who's not the concubine of a white man. There's not an old plantation on which the grandchildren of the owner are not whipped in the fields by the overseer."

Yet there were always a few whites who took better care of their Black children. They freed them, sent them to school, and tried to see that they got on in the world. Eventually these mulattos, quadroons, octaroons, and others of undefinable mixture formed a caste of their own, somewhere in between the underclass slaves and the free whites. Although many tried to enter the white world, only those who were light enough to disappear succeeded.

Until a few years ago, it was possible in most cases to tell what church a colored person went to by the depth of his color. Churches attended by the lighter-skinned population were known as "blue-veined" churches. There were also schools, colleges, and universities which were reserved almost exclusively for this half-caste population.

These people were separated because the rewards given to them tended to alienate them from their brothers below just as much as they were alienated from the white society above. So the only other course open to them was to remain distinct and apart. By color, class, and mentality they were neither white nor Black. Even today they are often like their ancestors who formed the Brown Fellowship Society in Charleston, South Carolina, in 1790. This organization admitted only people of intermediate racial status. It maintained a school, a clubhouse, and a cemetery. It provided assistance for widows and their children. One rule of this fellowship forbade all discussion of slavery; they just didn't want to be reminded.

This kind of attitude has been somewhat typical of all three groups in the Black middle class. Many of these people had struggled so hard to escape from the ghetto, pushed themselves so fiercely to achieve the tenuous status provided by middle class luxuries and surroundings, that their Black past, their Black people, even their own Black skins, had become their enemies. So they strove to erase their past, tried to break all contacts with their people, and yearned even to deny the blackness in themselves. Many of them would leave an integrated neighborhood as soon as "too many niggers" moved in.

They were much like the typical second-generation European immigrants who tried to escape the old-world ways and greenhorn styles of their parents. Because of this compulsion, the Black middle class was largely devoid of culture, even in the anthropological sense. They had renounced the folk culture from which they originated, yet they were unable to enter, or truly understand, the dominant culture which lured them.

The Black middle class was therefore left with nothing to guide their lives except *propriety,* as defined by the mass media—a confused and maladaptive mixture of sex and sanctity, prurience and puritanism, maudlin senti-

nentality, and blatant money-grubbing. So they struggled to emulate this model and to gain entrance to the
overclass.

Yet however they pursued this effort it was in vain.
They became the tokens of token integration, the social
elitists of the out class, lonely freaks in an alien world.
Or, worse yet, they were used as tools of white power
for the manipulation of their own people, as so many
Negro politicians, policemen, social workers, and intel-
lectuals have been. This kind of manipulation has, in
fact, been the traditional function of the Black middle
class. During the years of slavery, the surest path to
manumission was to betray a Black uprising. And even
today the most certain method of gaining recognition
from whites has been to become their agent in control-
ling the Blacks.

In the South, one of the main roles of the Black middle
class has been to deny publicly the existence of any
"Negro problem," especially on ceremonial occasions
such as the opening of a school when whites were
present. This performance was a basic technique for
securing favors from the whites. Sometimes it became
opportunistic; often it was simply the best thing a man
could do for his people; almost always, it was the price
of life.

But this role became so engrained in many of the
Black middle class that they were unable to escape it.
Even now there are many who join in white irrationality
concerning the Black community. For example, when
white people find filth in the streets of their neighborhood they quite properly call city hall and complain,

25

and it is removed. They know that the streets are sup posed to be cleaned by those who are paid to do it. But when the same whites (and warped Blacks) find filth in the ghetto streets, they call for a clean-up campaign by ghetto residents. This is obvious racism on the part of whites. But what could we call it on the part of Blacks who joined it? And how were we to bring such people into The Movement?

This problem was partially solved because many of the initial gains of The Movement went directly to the Black middle class. Since so many of these people were underemployed rather than unemployed, it was they who benefited when The Movement began opening up jobs and equalizing pay scales.

In 1964, the Small Business Administration reviewed its past ten years and reported that it had made seven loans to Blacks during that time—seven in ten years. This record is typical of most banks, savings and loan companies, and other financial institutions which provide the capital that allows people to enter the commercial world.

The Movement has had some success in breaking down this sort of discrimination, and many middle class Blacks have directly benefited. In this way they have been brought into The Movement, seeing that their self-interest was better served by being *with* Blacks than against them or aloof.

Yet we knew that these people would eventually have to be won to struggle at a higher level, with commitment not only to themselves but to all their brothers. Curiously, it was only when whites started joining The Movement in large numbers that middle class Blacks came too. It seemed that whites gave the struggle the sanction of authority. This in itself told us that the values of the Black middle class would have to be changed.

5

Program for the Nation

The third goal we saw was that our efforts must be directed toward changing the values of the entire nation. As Gunnar Myrdal pointed out over twenty years ago in his classic study *An American Dilemma,* this country does not have a Negro problem, it has a white problem. Changing the white majority, their attitudes and their institutions, is basic to any solution to "racial strife."

We saw that The Movement could free the Black population from its fear and misery only by freeing the white population from its hatred and guilt. We saw that we would have to face white society and force it to accept us, or we would have to reject its Christianity; force it to accept us, or we would have to reject its laws; force it to accept us, or we would have to reject its finest traditions.

We saw that the failure to admit Blacks to the society had created a permanent ambivalence within the nation, an ambivalence which warped everything the nation did. Even the simple facts of history had been so twisted that it was impossible for most Americans to understand what had happened to their land or why they had arrived at the crisis they were facing.

The nation's refusal to admit the humanity of Blacks had been accompanied by distortions of history and suppressions of fact. The role which Blacks had played in the development of the nation had been systematically falsified, both in schoolbooks and in academic history. For example, the first permanent non-Indian settlers in what is now the United States were not whites seeking religious freedom but Blacks seeking physical freedom. These people came here as slaves with an ill-fated Spanish colonial venture. They rebelled and sought refuge with the Indians. The Spanish eventually left, and the Blacks remained. This took place more than a hundred years before the landing of the Mayflower. It is also a fact that the first martyr of the American revolution was a Black man, Crispus Attucks, leader of the patriots who were killed by British soldiers in the Boston Massacre.

But facts such as these are of minor importance. They are merely historical trivia which are automatically excluded from most books. Of major importance, however, is the fact that at the time of the Revolutionary War the entire American economy was sustained by slavery. Slaves were held in every colony. The Northern industries such as shipbuilding and distilling were dependent on slave-grown agricultural products of the South. Northern trade, commerce, finance, and insurance all relied on the economic resources of the slavocracy.

The basis of American shipping at that time was the "triangular trade" in slaves, rum, and sugar. Sugar came from the West Indies to New England where it was made into rum. The rum was taken to Africa and traded for slaves. The slaves were brought to the West Indies in exchange for sugar. And the sugar again went to New England distilleries. Many of the slaves were only

29

"seasoned" in the West Indies and later came to the mainland, where half a million people were held in chattel bondage by the slavemasters who decided to go to war under the declaration that all men were created equal.

This initial ambivalence was made perfectly clear in the year 1787. It was then that Congress passed the Northwest Ordinance, specifically forbidding slavery in any states which might eventually be carved from the Northwest Territory. Yet, in the same year, the Constitutional Convention accepted the institution of slavery in the most fundamental document of American civilization.

One of the main reasons for the ambivalence concerning slavery during those early years was the fact that it was rapidly becoming unprofitable. The price of slaves was falling below the cost of their upkeep. But the invention of the cotton gin reversed this trend. Cotton became king of the South. The price of slaves soared. And since the South retained its control over American politics and government, cotton was the sovereign which held the entire nation in slavery.

For Blacks were not the only ones oppressed by slavery. Whites were also brutalized by their inability to escape from slavery. They kept themselves "up to their necks in the mud, trying to hold the dog down." In the South this was especially clear. A police state was created and the entire population lived in terror of a slave uprising.

Psychologically, this left millions of Americans suffering from misplaced hatreds. The classic example is the poor white Southerner who has been pitted against

Blacks by the powerful men who exploit them both. As long as these whites have had their insecurities and frustrations channeled into hatred for Blacks, they have been incapable of even perceiving their true plight, let alone attacking the real sources of their misery.

Yet until the second quarter of the nineteenth century, most of the antislavery agitation in the United States came from poor whites in the South. These people saw that slavery also kept *them* in bondage by allowing planters to control all the best land and manipulate the markets to their own advantage. In 1827, out of 130 antislavery groups in the United States, 106 were composed of poor whites in the South. But the movement which these societies represented was taken as an attack on private property—and crushed.

In opposition to the grass-roots abolitionists, John Calhoun voiced the typical slaveowner's view when he said that freedom for whites was impossible without the enslavement of Blacks. In the Dred Scott decision of 1857, the Chief Justice of the Supreme Court, Taney, gave legal sanction to this doctrine even in personal relationships, declaring that "a Negro has no rights which a white man need respect." The Court explained that the phrase "the people of the United States" in the Constitution was never meant to include Blacks. And this of course was perfectly correct.

The national ambivalence continued with pro- and antislavery agitation which became one of the direct causes of the Civil War. But this war too is largely misunderstood today. Schoolbooks often foster the impression that the North fought for the purpose of freeing

31

the slaves. Yet Lincoln specifically said that the question of slavery was irrelevant, that the war was being fought solely to save the Union.

It should also be remembered that there were slave states which fought with the Union. And, what is most convincing, it must be recalled that the Emancipation Proclamation was not made until the *third* year of the war. Nor did this proclamation affect the status of slavery in the loyal border states, or even in those areas of the South which had already come under federal control. The Great Emancipator's proclamation was simply an act of military necessity aimed at the rebels.

In 1862, when Lincoln first gave a draft of the Proclamation to his cabinet, Secretary of State Seward said, "It may be viewed as the last measure of an exhausted government, a cry for help, the government stretching out its hand to Ethiopia, not Ethiopia stretching forth her hand to the government." And that was certainly the truth of the matter. The government was in dire need of manpower and morale. It needed a reason to go on fighting and men to fight with. Eventually, two hundred thousand Blacks were mustered into the federal forces.

Given the fact that military expediency was the moving force behind the Emancipation Proclamation, it is not surprising that even after the War, America was unable to deal with the newly freed men as equals. At that time there was not even a plan to make them citizens, only free laborers. President Andrew Johnson, who took office after Lincoln's death, was against suffrage for Blacks on the grounds that it would make them the political equals of poor whites.

In fact, once the war was over, the North did not know what to do with the Black population. The war ended while Congress was out of session; and before they could return to pass laws the Southern legislatures reconvened and acted. They each passed some form of "Black Code" which laid down rules for governing the freedmen.

In Mississippi, for example, the code prohibited Blacks from owning land; required them to carry passes at all times; specified that if they violated a labor contract they forfeited all back pay; stated that Blacks without employment were legally "vagabonds," a crime which was punishable by fine, or, if the fine could not be payed, by a sentence of labor to a white man. Furthermore, any Black who left his employment could be apprehended by *any* white man and returned to his lawful employer. This was emancipation in Mississippi.

But when Congress came back into session these codes were struck down. The Republicans who controlled the national legislature had, for a variety of reasons, other ideas about what should be done. They created the Freedmen's Bureau, an agency designed to make the ex-slaves participants in the national economy. Much good work was done by the Bureau. Land which had come under government ownership was sold to Blacks. The basic rights of the ex-slaves were protected in contract arrangements with whites. A school system was set up. In doing these things, however, the Bureau won the fierce and everlasting enmity of white Southerners while, unfortunately, mishandling many of its legitimate duties. It lasted only seven years, until 1872. In a sense, it was given up in the compromise which created the Fifteenth Amendment.

In this amendment, the government officially forbade the denial of voting rights because of "race, color, or previous condition of servitude." And having done this, the government washed its hands of the whole matter, handing the implementation of this high-minded pronouncement over to the former slavemasters—a gambit which we have seen reenacted many times since then with civil rights legislation.

The white Southerners then passed laws such as those containing the "grandfather clauses." These simply stated that you could vote if your grandfather could, and if he couldn't, then neither could you. For ex-slaves and their children, this was simple, wholesale disenfranchisement. And these laws stayed on the books until the 1930s. In spite of their absence today, many of them are still enforced.

In addition, there were strong civil rights laws passed by the Republicans in Congress who wanted to break the hold of the Democratic party in the South. But soon the Republicans found other allies and abandoned the Blacks.

Most of the civil rights laws were struck down within ten years after the Civil War by a reactionary Supreme Court. One of the Court's decisions, for example, interpreted the Fourteenth Amendment as granting the privileges of national citizenship, but not necessarily state citizenship. This gave Blacks rights such as access to the seaports, but left questions of education, suffrage, and employment up to the states.

So for less than ten years after the Civil War, Blacks enjoyed the rights of citizenship. Then the dark ages came. Federal troops were withdrawn from the South in the compromise which gave Hayes the presidency after his disputed election with Tilden. And when the federal troops were gone Blacks were once again at the untender mercies of their former masters. During the 1890s, two to three Blacks were lynched every week—week after week, year after year. This period saw Senator Tilden of South Carolina publicly advocate the slaughter of Blacks in his state. He told a public gathering that he could not even remember how many Blacks he had killed.

During the Jim Crow mania of these years, states, counties, towns, and cities vied with one another in passing repressive legislation, running all the way from the silly to the insane, and often meeting, as when Birmingham, Alabama, prohibited Blacks and whites from playing checkers together. This was the period during which the "separate but equal" doctrine was taking shape. The results of that movement can still be seen in the South where rural gas stations often have three doors along the side labeled *Men, Women,* and *Colored*—separate but equal.

And so, as the years became decades and the decades became generations, millions of Blacks lived out their lives technically free, but still in slavery, without rights or legal recourse.

The Fifteenth Amendment, which guaranteed voting rights, was passed in 1870. Section two of that forty-six-word amendment stated that "the Congress shall have power to enforce this article by appropriate legislation." Ninety-five years later, in 1965, the Congress finally made use of the power it had reserved to itself. The Civil Rights Act of 1965 was intended partly to enforce the Fifteenth Amendment, because no more than a tiny fraction of the Black population had ever actually been allowed to vote.

Ninety-five years had elapsed before any attempt was made to enforce the Fifteenth Amendment. And in 1969 the Nixon administration attempted to remove this enforcing legislation which has just begun to change the complexion of the Southern electorate.

In 1957, soldiers of the First Airborne Division were sent to take nine Black children into Little Rock High School. This was the first time since the Hayes Compromise that the federal government had used force to protect the rights of Blacks in the South. In explaining the use of the troops, Eisenhower based his argument not on moral grounds but on legalisms and the threat of successful Communist propaganda if the children were not admitted.

In 1947, the President's Committee on Civil Rights said: "The pervasive gap between our aims and what we actually do is creating a kind of moral dry rot which eats away at the emotional and rational bases of democratic beliefs." This is the same ambivalence that has dogged America from the beginning. For, ironically, it is America's firm commitment to equalitarian ideals which makes the race question so intense. If Americans were not, in general, devoted to these ideals, they would not react so furiously while trying to accommodate the inconsistences between fact and ideal which the Black condition exposes.

In 1968, the Kerner Commission stated: "This is our basic conclusion: the nation is moving toward two societies, one Black, one white—separate and unequal." But this is really nothing new; this is where America has always been. Separate but unequal has always been the American experience for Blacks, an experience which has finally led us to question everything about America.

For example, Blacks today *must* ask themselves if and why they should go five thousand miles across the ocean to kill other colored people to defend a freedom they do not possess in their own land. And from that question it is an easy step to another, to asking if America's concern with freedom anywhere can be any more sincere than it has proven to be with its Black population at home.

One answer to this question appeared some time ago on a button worn by many young men in the ghetto. It said simply, "No Vietcong ever called me nigger!" This poignant phrase reveals the American ambivalence from the Black's point of view. We are asked to accept the responsibilities of citizenship without receiving the rights or rewards of that citizenship.

So we could see when we began our planning that a change in the nation's values must be one of our primary goals. We could see that what began as a Negro rights movement and became a civil rights movement would have to become a human rights movement encompassing the entire nation. It would not be enough even for the nation to change its attitudes and actions toward Black people—we saw that the nation would have to change its attitudes toward itself as well. White people as individuals and as a group would have to examine and redefine themselves, their past, and their future just as Blacks were doing. For only in this way could the goals of The Movement and the purposes of the entire nation be met.

6

A New Method

So we could see that the condition of the Black masses had to be changed, that the values of the Black middle class had to be changed, and that the direction of the entire nation had to be changed. And we could see that in order to finally accomplish these things we would have to find a new method of social action—a method that would cement our people together and generate the force to make them effective.

Considering the condition of our people, we knew that we had to find a method that would allow them to act in spite of fear. For they were genuinely and legitimately afraid. We had to find a method that used nothing external, for we were without resources beyond our bodies and our determination. And we had to find a method that would be dramatic enough to clearly demonstrate our cause, for we needed to gain real and immediate results.

We could see that a revolution was necessary, a revolution that would raise the bottom layer of American society to full citizenship. But we could also see that a cowed and crippled minority could not rise up suddenly and change the nation.

Looking back over four hundred years of American history, we saw protests, uprisings, revolts, pleas, and petitions—all of which had been fruitless. The Black condition remained essentially unchanged. A new style of movement had to be developed, a style that came from our own context, a style basic to our condition.

A way had to be found that would bring us allies, from our own people and from white society as well. And we knew that it would be difficult if not impossible for most whites even to understand our movement because they did not understand the conditions under which we lived. Every man thinks out of his own experience; no one can understand what he has never known. And few whites knew the Black condition. The Black population had been hidden away in ghettos, like an insane aunt chained in a barn loft so no one would see her, so the decent members of the family would not be embarrassed by her presence.

There were frequent references to the Black minority; the ex-slaves remained a scar on the nation's conscience, a sore in the nation's unconscious. Yet almost every public pronouncement concerning the condition of Blacks insisted that their situation was rapidly improving. But since Blacks were invisible to the white world, these questionable statements went unverified. Publicity was therefore of the highest strategic importance to any method we might choose. It was necessary to counter the overwhelming ignorance on the part of whites concerning the world in which we existed.

We could also see that our method must be different from those that had been used before—unsuccessfully. Some of our leaders had, for example, recommended movement through education; and we tried education—

we were *still* trying it. But the schools open to us were so poor, and the opportunities available to us after graduation were so meager, that we found we could not ameliorate our condition through education.

Other leaders recommended that we devote ourselves to industrial occupations; and we tried that. But we were retained only at the lowest levels of industry, and then only during the best of times. We were discriminated against by unions and management alike, unable to gain security through promotion or seniority.

Others recommended that we demand nothing, but simply give ourselves over to the goodwill of white generosity. And we tried that; we were *forced* to try that. For centuries, Uncle Tom went hat-in-hand to the back door of the white house to beg favors for his people. And, for centuries, this style had been both futile and emasculating. All that was given was restriction, and all that was gained was remorse.

Still other leaders counseled violence. And throughout the history of America, we fought many times, both in and out of the national armies. Before emancipation there were over 250 slave conspiracies and revolts. Blacks were prominent in the winning of the Revolutionary War; and many of them believed that they would gain their freedom then. Later, Blacks were the key to the Northern success in the Civil War; and freedom was actually promised at that time. But freedom never came. And in response to the continued lynchings and other forms of brutality, Blacks rioted, raided, and extracted vengeance many times. But none of this brought us any closer to release.

Throughout their history in America, both as individuals and as a group, Blacks have always faced the same cruel dilemma: whether to allow themselves to be destroyed slowly by the conditions which were imposed upon them, or to strike back and be destroyed quickly by the reaction that would follow. Recalling this, we knew we would have to find a method that would avoid both of these pitfalls, a method that would free us from the slow destruction without bringing on the quick.

The one method we found to answer all these needs was the method of nonviolent force. To some, nonviolence was merely a tactic, a discipline which was expected to provide certain advantages. To others it was a way of life, an end as much as a means. To all who accepted it, nonviolence offered new power. It pitted calm courage against frantic fear. It set the action of love against the reaction of hate.

Nonviolence was directed at immediate goals such as desegregation. It addressed itself to specific local enemies and attempted to force them to accede by recruiting their own conscience against them. At the same time, it was directed at the nation as a whole, in an attempt to reach the collective conscience that formed the national purpose, to establish a new basis for common good, for commonwealth.

Nonviolence became a form of Christian witness to the facts of intolerance, a form which forced others to witness, forced the nation to *see*. It was a petition which either succeeded immediately or became a national drama in which the injustice that made the petition necessary was reenacted.

This method of nonviolence was thus valuable because it exposed the lies which hid Blacks from whites. It made whites see the evils which flowed from intolerance. It made them see that the Blacks were constantly under the control of people who were psychologically incapable of allowing us to walk down the street in peace.

Nonviolence spoke to the value needs of Blacks and to the value dilemmas of whites. For as whites of goodwill wavered between their democratic ideals and the actuality of our enslavement, their goodwill was nullified, leaving the forces that openly defied democracy in complete control. For their sakes, as well as ours, these whites had to be forced to pursue their ideals actively.

One reason nonviolence was so electrifying to the nation was that America did not understand the way it operated. Nonviolence sought to move through sacrifice, to win through love. Those who wished to attack us found this enormously unfair. It increased their rage a thousandfold, for they perceived that their attacks would only make our success more certain.

The police moving into a demonstration with clubs knew, however dimly, that even if we were annihilated we would win for our cause. The more we lost personally, the more we gained for The Movement. This angered our enemies because it forced them at times to act with restraint. Then their fury became pent up and redoubled, so that when they attacked again it was with even greater intensity. And each time we were attacked, our allies, our numbers, and our determination increased.

As it confounded our enemies, this new discipline of nonviolence also provided satisfaction for our own deepest need—the need to see ourselves as human beings, as effective and substantial men and women with promise. So nonviolence was a method which at once began to end the old and create the new.

Finally, nonviolence appealed to us because the ends we sought by this method were inherent in the means we chose. And even as nonviolence forced us to risk our lives for the changes we desired, that risk itself made our lives more worth living.

The Birmingham campaign of 1963 was the first large-scale test of the new method. It was titled "Project C"— C for *confrontation*. Birmingham was chosen because it was believed to be the toughest city in the nation. This was a city which had closed its public parks rather than integrate them. During the six years prior to our campaign there had been seventeen unsolved bombings of Black churches and the homes of civil rights leaders in Birmingham. So we believed that if the method would work there it would work anywhere.

The campaign began slowly, with small marches and demonstrations to back up a list of demands which the city officials and businessmen of Birmingham had refused to accept. But the marches grew until almost twenty-five hundred demonstrators were in jail at one time. And every day more came, recruited by both the joys and the terrors of the struggle.

There were the joys of those who had never before stood up and defied the ancient cruelties which had scarred their lives. But there were terrors too, for each day we marched out of the yellow brick church to go downtown, and never got there. Two blocks away at the edge of the ghetto were the barricades where we were attacked by Bull Connor's police and firemen with dogs, clubs, and high-pressure hoses. We saw the heads of our brothers, sisters, wives, and children split by sticks, their flesh gnawed by wolfish dogs, their bodies spun skittering across the pavement by the force of the hoses. Night after night we went to bed knowing that the same drama would be reenacted when the sun rose.

Yet day after day we re-formed in the yellow brick church and marched out singing. And each day, as the repression mounted, our determination grew. Each day the clubbings were more furious, the dogs more viciously used, and the pressure of the hoses increased until their force peeled bark off the trees. But each day more people joined us. Each day there were more who could no longer stand and watch. Young people joined us by the thousands, emptying the schools to take up the challenge. Even whites joined. Finally our numbers were so great that we simply could not be contained. There were not enough police and firemen to stop us, and we surged past the barricades into downtown Birmingham as into the promised land.

At this point the city began "serious negotiations." When it became clear that we would not be crushed, official Birmingham relented and accepted our demands —a simple four-point program calling for (1) desegregation of all public facilities, (2) hiring and upgrading of workers without discrimination, (3) the release of all jailed demonstrators, and (4) the establishment of a permanent biracial committee to keep communications open between Blacks and whites.

This settlement drove segregationist whites into a fury. Bull Connor denounced the proceedings and called for a white boycott of any merchants who complied with the agreement. At a Klan rally one speaker shouted, "King should be met with force. King and Kennedy are worse than Castro. We need to go back to the old-time religion time, and the old-time Klan time."

That night, the headquarters of Project C were bombed. The home of the Rev. A. D. King, one of the leaders of the campaign and a brother of Martin Luther King, was bombed. The Black community reacted and a riot erupted which destroyed a large section of the city. President Kennedy quickly called troops into position nearby. But there was no more immediate violence. The confrontation in Birmingham was temporarily over. Project C had illuminated both the problems and the promise of nonviolence.

7

All the Way Home

The fifth goal of our movement was that we go all the way. Once we began, there was to be no turning back. We depended on mass support; the mobilization of our people was our principal weapon. The Movement only moved when we could attract large numbers who were willing to take great risks. If we failed, everyone who joined us would be open to retribution. If we failed, our people would be defenseless.

We had seen the defeat of other movements and had watched the repression which followed. We did not believe that our people could or would endure another such blow. To many, this seemed to be the last desperate attempt.

And we could see that insofar as America was not progressing toward the goals of democracy, it was regressing. Our activism was encouraging the activity of those who most violently opposed us. The nation was being polarized by Black demands, and people were being forced to choose. The best could no longer pretend that the worst were ineffective; they could no longer mouth liberal sentiments and still accept reactionary conditions.

We were continually warned about "backlash"—which is what white people do when Black people fail to "stay in their place." We were continually told by whites and fearful Blacks alike that we were fomenting discord, creating racial strife, mounting reaction and bigotry. Sometimes this warning came as an unvarnished threat in the nature of, "You do and I'll kill you!" At other times the threat was veiled, saying, in effect, "Well, if you do that, I wash my hands of the whole matter, and you'll deserve whatever you get."

Most often the warning came from people who truly believed they were our friends, people who were gripped by the fear that we would set the "Negro cause," as they saw it, back endless years by our impatience. These people were usually whites who had appointed themselves Negro leaders, whites who were setting their own timetable for Black freedom, putting it off for the future when everyone would be ready for it.

In this case, "everyone" included the most fanatic bigots. So this attitude took for granted that the sensitivity of sick racists should provide the framework in which we moved, that the paranoia of white supremicists should be granted legitimacy above our aspirations for freedom, that segregationists should be allowed to set the limits of the liberty we would enjoy.

White liberals who accepted this attitude usually had a personal stake in the game they were playing. Most often, they had been acting as spokesmen for the Black community and now pointed to the accomplishments that had been made under their guidance. But once we investigated, these accomplishments proved illusory.

It is true that there were Black ballplayers in the major leagues. There were token Blacks in the political, business, and military establishments. Some colleges had raised their pitifully small quotas; and a few schools had been forced to accept a few Black children. But the great mass of Black Americans were still being tortured.

Yet the Black press had been partially responsible for perpetuating the myth of progress. In their search for something to hold on to, Blacks had learned to satisfy themselves with whatever they could find. And with real accomplishments so scarce, imagination had to be added liberally. Thus, the hiring of one Black airline pilot, the academic success of one Black student, the promotion of a Black military officer—each of these was treated as if it heralded the dawning of a new day. But, in fact, these were the exceptions that proved the rule.

As John F. Kennedy said, "A Negro baby born in America today, regardless of the section or state in which he is born, has about one-half as much chance of completing high school as a white baby born in the same place, on the same day—one-third as much chance of completing college—a third as much chance of becoming a professional man—about one-seventh as much chance of earning $10,000 a year—a life expectancy which is seven years less—and the prospects of earning only half as much." The President might have added that the Black baby had only two-thirds as much chance of even living to be a year old. But the point is simply that these statistics offer a far more adequate description of the Black condition than do the few highly publicized Blacks who manage to escape the condition which these statistics describe.

White liberals also touted the success gained through legal action. But important as some court battles have been, they failed to make any basic change in the lives of most Blacks. For example, all statistics show that in spite of the long, patient, and costly legal battle against segregation in the schools, segregation is actually increasing.

The first of the series of lawsuits aimed at desegregating schools was won in 1935 when Thurgood Marshall persuaded the Maryland Court of Appeals to order the state to admit Donald Murry to its university. Today, thirty-five years later, despite hundreds of such victories, the job is just beginning. Most of the cases have gained no more than token compliance. And Southerners have pledged themselves to a "century of litigation" to block efforts at breaking down segregation through the courts.

Ten years after the school desegregation cases of 1954, only 2.14 per cent of the nearly three million Black children in Southern schools had been affected and were receiving anything like a desegregated education. Today, fifteen years after the 1954 decision, the President of the United States has even attempted to eliminate the deadlines for compliance as being unrealistically harsh, although the Supreme Court is insisting on speed. By now, over a million Black children have gone from kindergarten through high school in segregated inferiority *since* the Court decided that Blacks had a right to a decent education. And there are hundreds of thousands more children entering the same system each year.

To a large extent it was the ineffectiveness of these legal measures, especially the school desegregation acts and subsequent litigation, that led the younger generation of Blacks to activism and protest. And as this protest reached massive proportions it became clear that those Americans who were not coming to realize the justice of the Black demands were closing their minds more permanently and more desperately to justice. We could see that insofar as America was not liberalizing its laws and more aggressively implementing those laws already passed, racism was becoming more highly institutionalized, more widespread, and more brutal.

We realized, too, that this was unavoidable. For there was a truth to those warnings delivered by our liberal friends. It was not true that everything was going along all right before our agitation began; that was a simple lie. Nor was it true that we wanted too much too fast; our patience had long since degenerated into collaboration with our oppression. But it *was* true that massive opposition was stirring in reaction to The Movement.

White citizens' councils were forming throughout the South. The Klan was recruiting and spreading. Lester Maddox was beginning his campaign for governor by passing out ax handles. The American Nazi Party was stockpiling weapons and hatred. In the Northern cities, the names were sometimes different but the motives were the same whether they came under the heading of parents' and taxpayers' groups, homeowners' associations, or community school councils.

The growth of such organizations made it clear that the drive we were beginning must take us all the way.

The opposition which had arisen was obviously planning to go all the way with its efforts. It clearly intended that no improvement should be made in our lives. But Blacks were no longer willing to accept this fate. A new mood was growing. There was a spirit of "liberty or death." And as the ultimate confrontation came into view, it was clear that if our movement did not succeed, did not go all the way, Black and white America would fail together.

Part III

THE OLD ASSUMPTIONS

8

Prologue to the Past

After fifteen years of struggle, the wall of ignorance, superstition, intolerance, and violence remains. And now The Movement is taking on new direction. But before we can lay a course toward the future with any assurance of success we must examine closely the reasons for our failure in the past. We must discover how we came to be where we are.

When the present struggle began, it had no formal ideology to describe the changes it sought or the ways in which it moved toward those changes. The Movement sprang from Christian morality, and its strategy and tactics evolved from that morality. The strategic goals could be defined in terms of the New Man and the New World which the apostle Paul proclaimed two thousand years before. The tactics could be explained in terms of Christian witness, Christian witness moved out of the pews and the pulpits and into the streets. That was how nonviolent action began.

Now the question is, Why did it fail to deliver freedom for Black people? In order to understand this, we must investigate some of the underlying assumptions that made it seem workable at the time. For example, we assumed that integration was the model for our success. We assumed that the barriers of segregation would be broken when enough good men saw the justice of our cause. We assumed that we were dealing with an open, democratic, and Christian nation, a nation which *had*, and would, implement the solutions to our condition. And we assumed that a single ideology of movement would be sufficient to our success.

Each one of these assumptions was taken from white America's description of itself. They are basic presuppositions about the nature of American society. Altogether they show how completely the Black subculture accepted the pronouncements of the dominant majority. But in our action we proved each of these pronouncements false. And, as this happened, we came closer to a definition of America which would allow us to operate effectively. But *until* this happened we were impotent. As long as we believed what the nation said about itself we chose strategies which in no way corresponded to the reality we faced, strategies which were bound to fail. The fall of these assumptions changed most of our strategies and many of our tactics. But our original objectives remain. The goals we saw in the beginning still lie ahead, still far off. Yet we have come a long way, in many respects a tragically long way. We have traveled from the bloody heroism of Birmingham to the burning of Chicago, and we have arrived at a new beginning.

We can only look back with pained nostalgia at those grand days such as the one on which men and women from across the nation gathered in a small Black church in Selma, Alabama, to declare their oneness in God before marching out to meet the repressive power of a dictatorial state. These people had come to assert their faith in America's possibilities, to proclaim the American dream as their own, and to affirm that the finest ideals of that dream could become reality in Selma, Alabama. All of the people gathered there shared our assumptions.

We acted together on those assumptions that day and for years of hopeful days to follow. But neither time nor trust brought us closer to our goals. Although we won many battles, we never tasted the fruits of victory. Our accomplishments often bewildered us as much as our defeats.

We would achieve the removal of some discriminatory legislation, only to find that discrimination continued. We would win the passage of a new law, only to see it go unenforced. Then we wavered, no longer secure on the foundation we had laid. We began to question our assumptions, to clarify them as we acted, to act with these assumptions more clearly in mind.

As each new effort was crowned with thorny failure, we learned from our loss. Action and reaction convinced us of the fallacies in our assumptions. Failure upon failure taught us that these assumptions must be discarded.

Still, it was not until the riots began that we understood the extent of our failure. The message from the streets was that hundreds of years of Black appeals for justice would now give way to action. We had to face the truth that the land was without justice, and that our strategies based on appeals for justice were bound to fail. For justice, by definition, is fair and evenhanded. When there is no justice for *all*, then there is no justice at all. Some may be favored, but none are safe.

The message from the streets was that too many had been suffering too much for too long, and that even The Movement was doing too little about it. In every city, store windows flaunted the wealth denied to Blacks. The mass media advertised the leisure, security, and comfort which were the American way of life—for whites. Under the pressure of these taunts, the massive force of untended grief and unanswered need broke through.

The language of Newark, Detroit, and Watts could not be avoided, nor could it be costumed in the language of the preacher, the negotiator, or the man of goodwill and selfless interest. Dick Gregory was shot trying to cool off the rebellion in Watts. Martin Luther King was stoned in Harlem. A new movement was taking shape.

The cities convulsed by riots finally showed us how deeply we had been lulled into the American dream, a rosy, foggy dream through which most of our countrymen are still sleeping. We have been rudely awakened now. We see a different American landscape, harsher, grimmer, but in the bold and somehow comforting relief of stern reality.

Yet it is never easy to give up cherished beliefs; and it is especially hard when the beliefs are sweet and the truth bitter. But it is good medicine. It was painful when our basic assumptions were stripped from us. We wanted to believe them. They were good to believe— too good.

But once these assumptions were gone we could look clearly at the facts. When we did this, we saw how the Civil Rights Movement was born. We were brought into it almost without knowing. We arrived at new beliefs even before we discarded the old. And the new beliefs were tempered by the heat of battle, hardened in the furnace of our failure. We had been bitterly rewarded for our old assumptions. But from that bitterness we now hope will come the understanding required for the creation of a society in which those old assumptions finally do hold true.

9

The New Separatism

The first and perhaps most fundamental assumption with which we began was that integration would be the route to Black freedom. And this was an inherent part of all our other assumptions. The concept of integration won our allegiance because it fit our understanding of how the people of a culture should relate to one another. It fit our understanding of the values which should determine the institutions and priorities of a society. It did not, however, fit American reality. And the measure by which we misjudged that reality is precisely the measure of the yawning gulf between Blacks and whites.

Almost everything we learned in The Movement makes integration impossible as a goal for the Black community today. Genuine integration can never become a reality until both parties can live together as equals; and that will not happen until each sees the other as human, until each holds the same values upon which the entire culture can grow.

So integration is dead. The concept and the experience, insofar as they were tried, have both failed because of the powerful racism of this society. Whites decided that integration was too high a price to pay for peace.

And Blacks, in response, have realized that they must develop their own distinctive culture.

Integration is dead, but Black people did not kill it. They *could* not because they were never in a position to do so. The Black minority has never had control of the concept or definition of integration.

In the integration model, the majority power is always the broker of the terms. In America, this has made the white liberal a bridge between the Black and white worlds. He thus became the leader of the Blacks, but he could not adequately fill this role because he had too little stake in Black freedom. He did not understand the depth of the Black needs. Nor did he understand the shallowness of his own commitment. For this reason, the integration model has always had a built-in obsolescence.

We see now that our movement not only must provide the minimal demands which are the rights of *all* people—enfranchisement, education, employment—but also must move beyond that to deal with the requirements which are unique to our people. At this point the articulation of goals absolutely requires a spokesman from the minority. Only someone whose very identity is founded on the sentiments, needs, and urgency of his people can validly and competently make known these further requirements.

A Black spokesman, if he is truly representative, cannot afford to waver or turn back at any point. A liberal-minded white may at any time decide that the process has gone far enough, that the Blacks have achieved all they need, that further demands are unreasonable or too costly. But the true minority representative will not, because he cannot, cease until his full status as a human being is affirmed and assured.

So, today, Black organizations and communities are ridding themselves of many erstwhile and questionable white friends. There has been a wholesale disaffection from the suburban ladies' groups that devote themselves to charity, the churches that dedicate themselves to home mission, the agencies, bureaus, and commissions that claim to deal with the Black condition. There are large-scale efforts to remove the machine politicians and other opportunists who stand between Blacks and an appropriate response from their government. All of these people are being told the same thing: they must either turn themselves over to Black control or remove themselves from the Black community.

All of these groups have claimed to speak for the Black communities which they pretend to serve. And their self-willed, self-defined, and self-righteous misunderstanding has added greatly to the confusion about what Blacks want and how serious they are about getting it.

Welfare organizations offer a clear example. The far-right groups who decry welfare as a waste of natural resources and the ruination of human dignity would likely be surprised to find that the strongest spokesmen for this point of view are to be found not in their own ranks but among those trapped as recipients of welfare. Black organizations that have organized around welfare have almost universally called for the abolishment of that system.

Who, then, really *wants* the welfare system? Who profits by it? Who perpetuates it? It is, of course, the people who *run* the system. They are the ones who really benefit, the ones with a vested interest in its perpetuation. It is those who *administer* welfare who get the most money, not the recipients; it is the administrators who are most truly *on* welfare. This point should always be remembered when they try to speak for the Black community.

This same phenomenon is repeated endlessly by every white group or white-controlled institution, such as churches and YMCAs, that attempts to explain the needs of Blacks. America must learn to stop listening to these self-appointed spokesmen. They have no solutions because they have no understanding. They have no understanding because they have personal interests which they are trying to preserve, interests which prevent them from seeing the true Black condition or hearing the actual Black demands.

The collapse of the integration model has led to many social experiments ranging from Black capitalism to the African revival. There has been a headlong search for new sources of identity. From the Black Muslims and the Black Jews to the Black Caucus within the Catholic priesthood, Black people have been led to a growing awareness of their distinctive needs. Basic to all of these is the obvious necessity for Blacks to join in the creation of a dialogue which will lead to an overall strategy for Black America.

Even within The Movement this has led to a new conception of "separate but equal." Very few integrated groups are being formed. Many thousands of whites have left Black organizations in order to form their own groups. In most cases these people began as white liberals who were devoted to helping solve the problems of Blacks. What these whites learned from their efforts was that the real problems lie within the white community, that *they*, the whites, have the real problem. This experience typically changed them from white liberals to white radicals, in the true sense of the term, the sense of going to the root of things. This change took place as they perceived the roots of the problems they sought to solve.

In other cases, Black movement organizations have found it necessary to expel their white members. In one sense this move was necessary because reliance on whites had left these organizations without support in the Black community. For, however well-meaning they were, these whites were basically incapable of representing their Black constituencies. There was too much ingrained suspicion of white members, and the need to have Black leaders only was too great. Blacks, like whites, need to trust and identify with their leaders, to feel free with and equal to them. Blacks, like whites, need leaders who are truly a part of the community they claim to represent, leaders who can be counted on because they are known in other capacities, who can be argued with because they have to respond.

This new separatism is visible at every level of Black society. Black caucuses are being formed not only in the churches but in labor unions, schools, colleges, universities, legislatures, political parties, and professional organizations. There are other manifestations as well: numberless new Black businesses, African import shops, Black bookstores, printing houses, dairies, department stores, banks, and building firms.

This new Black movement is largely a reaction to helplessness, to the divide-and-conquer tactics which have always been used against the Black population. It is a response to tokenism and to the failure of white America to provide the social, economic, and intellectual resources necessary for dealing with the Black condition. This particular response did not come sooner because Blacks had been concentrating their efforts on integration, on getting into the larger society rather than on perfecting their own.

Within Black communities, therefore, the cry is no longer for integrated education, but for community control. This means more than just decentralization. It means Black control of Black schools, just as whites have always controlled their schools. This demand has in some cases left racists comically trapped in their own "separate-but-equal" rhetoric, flabbergasted to hear themselves using the same arguments as Black militants. In a few cases there have even been beginning attempts at coalition between bigots and Blacks in opposition to the white liberals who refuse to give up the rubric of integration.

There is an exciting new mood within the new Black organizations. One can sense the relief which accompanies liberation from false presuppositions and false goals. One can sense the release of new energies and a new seriousness stemming from the knowledge that this nation will have to become concerned with its democratic values if it is going to make its own laws a reality.

One of the most interesting things is that those Black organizations which have accepted separatism most fully, such as the Black Panthers, are the ones who are now most capable of cooperating with white organizations in activities which happen to be to their mutual benefit. The Peace and Freedom Party campaign is a striking example.

Some segments of the Black movement are concerning themselves specifically with the creation and re-creation of Black culture. Others have found inspiration in such international movements as socialism. Still others have tried to preserve and extend what they consider to be the finest thought and ideals, the most humane traditions, of American civilization. All of these, however, have discovered that white America as it exists today is not something they want to be a part of. They do not want to be integrated into a sinking ship or a dying culture. There is disagreement about precisely what changes should be made. But there is no argument about the necessity for change or the direction which that change must take.

Separatism has taken the place of integration as the strategy and tactic of The Movement. It is tactically necessary in order to achieve the kind of unity needed to accomplish the aims of the Black community. It will also function as a strategy until those ends are met.

It is clear that those ends cannot be met short of the regeneration of the entire American society. And, barring that renewal, the only sanity seems to lie in a new form of segregation which will hopefully, in time, bring a new demand for integration—the integration of whites into the re-created culture that the Black minority has begun to achieve.

10

The Mask and the Man

Having assumed that integration would be the principle of our success, we accepted the corollary proposition that the basic hindrance we faced was legal segregation. We therefore directed our efforts to removing the laws which limited us and to creating new laws which would set us free. But as these things were in fact accomplished without bringing the freedom we sought, we began to see that we were dealing not with a legal matter but with a sickness, the disease of racism. This is the problem to which our energies must now be addressed.

The laws of the land merely reflect currents in the body politic. They are symbols and symptoms, not causes, of the national state of mind. And in the case of civil rights legislation, the laws often hide this state of mind more than they reveal it. They are more often ends than means. They are most often passed as a gesture and meant to remain unenforced.

We learned this as we found that legislation did not change our condition. After ten years of our movement, and a goodly amount of favorable legislation, the Black condition was growing worse. Each year after the historic 1954 school desegregation decision of the Supreme Court, more children found themselves in more

segregated schools. In spite of laws forbidding discrimination in employment, Black income was being steadily
reduced below subsistence levels.

Unemployment in Black communities was twice to
three times what it was in white communities; salaries
were about half. Regardless of government programs
and pronouncements concerning improvements in health
and welfare, infant mortality in the Black community
was almost twice as high among Blacks as it was among
whites. Malnutrition was rampant. Vitamin deficiency
diseases were almost typical. Disease, disorder, and de-
cay remained the constant companions of Blacks across
the land.

Eventually we realized that there were actually enough
laws on the books of this land to nullify every ruse of
bigotry if the nation had been willing to back the laws
up. But the laws were buried and ignored because this
was in fact the will of the majority. It became clear that
the best laws concealed rather than reflected the desires
of the people, and that the laws we cared most about
were first produced to appease liberal sentiments and
then forgotten to placate the reactionary.

The Fifteenth Amendment is a prime case in point.
Theoretically, this legislation gave Blacks the right to
vote. However, its passage was accompanied by an
agreement which removed federal troops from the South
and left the implementation of the amendment up to
individual states. This amendment, which our history
books tell us was a giant step forward for the Black
minority, was in fact a revocation of the few rights that
Blacks had been granted during Reconstruction, and a

signal that opened an era of unprecedented terrorism in which lynching became the true law of the land. The nation had produced a humane and progressive law. And, as a direct result of the means by which that law was passed, lynchings began to be advertised in newspapers before they occurred. Families came with picnic lunches on chartered trains for the festivities.

Racism is so fundamental to American life that laws have never been able to unsettle it. In order to understand this thoroughly, we must remember that in America racism is not just the natural distaste with which distinct cultures have usually viewed each other. The American brand of racism is something unique. American racism was born here and has existed nowhere else. It is entirely an American product.

The Blacks who were brought to America during the earliest colonial times did not encounter racism. In fact, though they were brought here and sold against their will, they were not sold as slaves, for slavery was unknown in America at that time. They were sold as indentured servants just as many thousands of whites were. And the Black indentured servants were apparently treated just as the whites were. Many individual masters tried to hold white servants in life slavery; but these attempts failed. The whites could always escape and blend in with the rest of the freemen; or they could appeal to their governments and get redress. There were also many attempts to enslave Indians. But Indians died off rapidly in confinement, or ran back to their people. In the end, the whites and reds were given up in favor of the Blacks.

When they first arrived, Blacks met no more social or legal discrimination than the whites who were kidnapped in Bristol or London and sold in America—certainly no more than the paupers, prostitutes, pickpockets, and tramps who were sentenced to servitude in America by English courts. After serving the period of their indenture, Blacks mingled freely with the rest of society. They voted, owned property, married, raised families, worked, lived, died, and were buried just as anyone else.

More than a generation passed before Blacks came to be thought of as ideal for slavery. It was then that laws were passed making their servitude permanent and inherited. Yet it is interesting to note that the first excuse used for enslaving them was not race but religion. They were considered fit for slavery because they were not Christians. This, however, was merely an excuse, as was shown when baptized Africans began showing up.

The important thing to remember is that America was not at this time a racist society. It was simply barbaric. It had tried to enslave everyone, but only the Blacks worked out. Yet this historical process eventually gave the nation much more than a peculiar economic institution. It implanted guilt and fear permanently in the American mind, where they have been festering for more than four hundred years to create the social disease of racism as we see it today.

Throughout the history of white America this guilt and fear have vied with the nation's democratic ideals to create the national ambivalence under which the Black man was compelled to live. There was never a time during slavery when antislavery sentiment was en-

71

tirely dead. Nor has there been a time since when the forces which sought to reduce Blacks completely have been quelled.

When Thomas Jefferson, himself a slaveowner, was forced to delete a passage condemning slavery from the Declaration of Independence, it was merely the first instance in the legislative portfolio of the land when conflict between high ideals and low motives found compromise at the expense of the Blacks. At that time slavery was big business. The slave-owning interests had become a major power bloc in the nation. And the process of slaveholding had been rationalized in the minds of the masters.

One of the earliest social manifestations of the slave society was the establishment of a national atmosphere of violence and terror. The slaves had somehow survived as men and women, even though legislation declared them subhuman. They survived to rebel. And the anger, fear, guilt, and resentment on the part of the whites at every sign of independence underlay the brutal laws which bound the slave. These laws were clearly made to sanction and support racism.

Yet the racism which brutalized the slave had a similar effect upon the master, for the man who desecrates the humanity of another destroys his own humanity as well. The effect of this viciousness was a nationwide brutality of spirit. Whether he owned slaves or not, every white American knew there was one class of people to whom normal standards of decency did not apply. Furthermore, that class had recourse neither to self-defense nor to law.

The white took for granted his unrestricted power in relation to the Black (even if he used it benignly) and this mind-set extended automatically to the rest of the colored world. The white man's relation to the Black in this country was mirrored by America's callous colonialism abroad.

The white man's relation to colored people, both domestic and foreign, was unrestricted by legality or morality. No code of justice operated between them. So by the time laws giving legal rights to Black people were created, the social structures, mores, and psychological bent of the nation were such that the laws did little more than whitewash the existing system of subordination.

Thus white America could never affirm universal humanity in practice even though it might do so in law. It acquired early the crippled conscience which made it *necessary* to pass laws against such things as lynching —even if the laws were not obeyed or enforced. The best white Americans have allowed themselves to watch passively what the worst have indulged in with sadistic glee.

The creation of a permanent subordinate caste left a deep scar on the American spirit. The Black was given a searing conviction of his own inferiority. Equally dangerous was the white's assumption of his own superiority without reference to qualification or achievement. Both of these mental habits had led to violence.

Throughout the history of emancipation, the Thirteenth, Fourteenth, and Fifteenth Amendments, and a hundred years of civil rights legislation, the pattern of illegal and accepted violence has endured, challenged only weakly during the last decade. This violence has been of two sorts. First, the psychological, social, and economic deprivation which imposed a steady erosion of spirit on Black people. Second, the continual overt physical violence in the form of beatings, lynchings, murders, and race riots.

The tradition of lynching has continued strong throughout the twentieth century. Men and women who had been granted the rights and privileges of citizenship by law were lynched for such crimes as leaving their jobs, testifying against whites in court, failing to say *Sir*, arguing over the price of berries, and accepting a job as postmaster.

Yet the nonviolent movement operated on the assumption that legal segregation was the real enemy and that it would be mitigated by law. We offered white society an opportunity to act in good faith, and we found that it would not. The hopes which our movement created and left unfulfilled contributed to the despair which eventually leapt to flames in the nation's ghettos.

The burning of the ghettos is a mammoth demonstration that Blacks understand thoroughly what liberal whites refuse to admit: that the unwritten laws of subjugation are more important to this nation than the written laws which oppose it. In fact, it has recently been discovered that many of the Reconstruction laws are more useful for prosecuting those who perpetuate discrimination than are the more recent civil rights acts. So lack of laws has never been our problem.

The problems of race and domestic peace are not problems of legislative program, although these may be important. They are problems of the will, problems of national priority, problems of the spirit. And they are problems which can no longer be avoided.

The reality of racism and the ways in which it operates against Black people have been thoroughly documented. But it was necessary for us to go through the long process of testing and discovering for ourselves before the legal mask was torn off the face of American bigotry. For then, without the support of law, the real hatred of whites for Blacks was forced out into the open. We began to deal face to face with the true enemy.

This discovery marked an important advance both for The Movement and for white America. It defined the problem more clearly than ever before. We can now see what will be necessary if we are going to live as one nation. Whites must work with themselves, to eradicate the sickness and rebuild the structures which are grounded in racism. And Blacks must work with themselves, to unite and deal with the real enemy. We can no longer fence with straw men in our battle for survival.

11

The System

We had discovered that the legal segregation we
attacked was solidly supported by racism. When we
won a battle against segregation, it was like tearing down
paper to expose the stone wall behind.

Our next assumption was that individual men could
change the system that oppressed us, could unlock the
gates of segregation and allow us to enter the society.
We believed that individuals—congressmen, judges, administrators, business leaders—had the power to deliver
us from bondage.

The Movement had first defined itself as a coalition of
Blacks with whites of goodwill, moving together to
effect change in segregated structures. We envisioned
that change occurring when those in positions of leadership in powerful political, economic, and social institutions were either convinced of the justice of our cause
or forced in spite of themselves to support us. We therefore sought to influence these men, to get them to do
what we thought we could not do ourselves. We assumed that these men *had* the power which in fact they
only represented.

And we learned that racism is not just an attitude of
individuals, but that it is also built into institutions as a
tradition, a code of conduct, an unwritten social contract.
We learned that *institutions themselves* can be racist,

regardless of who is running them. We learned, in fact, that all of the major institutions of American society have been created and developed in such a way as to discriminate.

The educational institutions of the nation may provide the best example of institutional racism. Education is one of the major keys to success in a technological society. But it is clear that Blacks have been far less successful in the academic world than whites. Blacks claim that this is a function of racism in the schools, but the current educational theories, produced by whites, offer another explanation. Terms such as "cultural deprivation" and "social disadvantagement" are used to account for the lower achievement of Black children.

According to the theories to which these terms refer, a large proportion of Black children are stultified by their early upbringing. These children allegedly receive such limited stimulation from their environment that they are permanently handicapped for academic pursuits. Blacks, however, say that this is no more than the old racial inferiority theory in modern dress, at best a replacement of racial prejudice with cultural and class prejudice. The old-fashioned theories held that Black children learned poorly because they were stupid. Modern theories hold that Black children learn poorly because they have been stupified by their upbringing. In other words, Blacks are not inferior as individuals, only as a group. This theory is also applied to poor whites and to other groups such as Puerto Ricans.

But if we look at how these theories are established we will see the effects of bias and prejudice. For example, on a standard IQ test, the child is asked verbally to circle a Christmas wreath which appears on a page with several other objects including a teakettle. It is assumed that a sensitive child will be able to recognize the wreath. But a child from a poor neighborhood where money for Christmas decorations is unavailable may never have seen such an object or had it named. For that matter, a child from a wealthy and intellectual Jewish community where Christmas is not celebrated may never have come in contact with a wreath. Is this, then, proof of cultural deprivation? Actually, it is only a proof of cultural *difference.*

The researchers ask questions which are culturally determined; and they have the arrogance to assume that unfamiliarity with *their* culture is ignorance. All they actually prove is that the children whom they label "culturally deprived" are from a different culture. And it should have been clear from the outset that most Black children have cultural backgrounds very different from those of most white researchers.

Yet the researchers offer other proof. They simply point to the academic records of Black children. And these certainly do show inferiority. The question is, What or whose inferiority do they show? If we examine the schools in which Black children study we will immediately begin to see where the inferiority lies.

In the ordinary Black school, the basic prerequisites for learning are absent. For example, it is clear that adequate learning can take place only where there is communication between teacher and child concerning the subject matter. And this can only happen when there is a controllable class size. Yet, whether we take national or most local statistics, we see that Black schools are greatly overcrowded and understaffed. Black schools, are, in fact, generally so crowded that even the best teachers spend most of their time simply keeping order. It is enormously instructive to watch someone try to teach forty-two five-year-olds to read, all at the same time. This is the definition of futility. And it turns good teachers into jailers.

All this makes all academic comparisons with white schools inapplicable. If the Black schools are inferior, nothing can be established about the inferiority of Black children by comparing their schoolwork with that of white children. A theory of cultural deprivation could be applied only where the basic conditions for learning are present and equal. In the absence of these conditions, such a theory is irrelevant.

Yet teachers and class size are not the only factors that affect learning. In the typical Black school many of the children are dulled by hunger. Others are racked by long-standing diseases or aching teeth which need medical attention that their families cannot afford. Others need glasses. And all of them live packed in Black ghetto tenements, and yet are given schoolbooks (when such are available) showing white Dick running over his green suburban lawn with his new red wagon and a puppy. This constitutes outrageous irrelevance in education.

From such a situation a child can learn only two things: aversion or obedience. And in many ways this seems to be the function of the school system where Blacks are concerned. The society is preparing them for life as passive menials, and such unruly instincts as creativity must be weeded out in this process. Conformity is the only index of success.

The brightest children are naturally driven out of this situation. Since they would make poor menials anyway, their loss means nothing to this system. An extensive survey on metropolitan America, prepared by the U. S. Commissioner of Education, shows the effects of this system. They cannot be emphasized too much. The facts show that the average intelligence of high school dropouts is higher than the average intelligence of high school graduates.

This statistic describes America better than anything else. America is a nation in which the average intelligence of high school dropouts is higher than the average intelligence of high school graduates. The best minds are being systematically driven from the schools. And in most Black schools even those who finish, those who learn to obey at the expense of having their finest potential crushed, do not really get anything which in a technological society can be called an education.

Kenneth Clark in his *Dark Ghetto*, a study of Harlem, cites the reading scores of children in ghetto schools as they go through their academic careers. He shows that each year they fall further behind, are moronized by their education, so that, upon graduation, even if their poverty does not prevent them from going on to college their education will.

It is for all these reasons that Blacks claim that both the schools and the theories which blame Black children instead of the schools are racist. Yet whites may insist

that Black schools are overcrowded only because Black
neighborhoods are overcrowded. Still, it is clear that
Black neighborhoods are overcrowded because of housing segregation, which is obvious racism.

Whites may argue that housing patterns are *economically* determined, that Blacks simply cannot move out
of the slums because they are poor. But even if this
were true it is obvious that the poverty is the result of
job and wage discrimination, which is obvious racism.
But, again, whites may claim that there is no *substantial*
job discrimination, that Blacks are simply unprepared
and unqualified for the many positions which are open
to them. But even if this were wholly true it would be
the result of inferior education, which is obvious racism.

So the circle of argument is closed. It ends where it
began—with an overworked teacher in an overcrowded
classroom. It ends where it began—with institutionalized
racism. And in the rare Black classroom where a good
teacher has a reasonable class size, no theory of cultural
deprivation will be applicable. For Black children will
be learning perfectly well.

Can anyone wonder that Blacks rebel, demanding
more and more vociferously that educational institutions
provide something which truly corresponds to their
needs? Can anyone wonder that a few men of goodwill
within these institutions are powerless to change the
cast and fabric of the organizations which employ them?
No executive fiat can remove a racism which is so deeply
engrained.

Nor is it only the schools which are so constituted.
The nation's institutions form a tightly interwoven

system which supports and perpetuates inequality. Individual whites of goodwill are as powerless against this system as we, the excluded. Yet it was not until we saw the structures in which these men lived and worked reject their voices that we learned that individuals, white or Black, cannot effect change in America.

Thousands of churchmen participated in our marches and protests, casting the weight of their power and prestige behind us. But their churches did not join them; they remained fortresses of bigotry.

Captains of industry supported us, donating their time, their money, and their expertise to our cause. But their corporations did not provide us with jobs.

Union leaders came forward to back us, issuing statements on our behalf and lending their organizing experience to help us gather our people to The Movement. But their unions did not remove racial barriers.

Government leaders gave us their approval, spoke for us, and worked behind the scenes in attempts to bring about our success. But their troops and police did not protect us from the continued exclusion of our constitutional rights.

So we learned that these individuals did not have the ability to change things. They did not have the power. The institutions in which they were operating were so petrified with prejudice that goodwill, even at the top, did not suffice to soften the effects of racism throughout. We also learned that the application of justice is a function of structures and institutions, not of man nor even of laws. Rather, it is the political and judicial institutions of the nation which mete out "justice" in accordance with tradition.

We found men of goodwill who were impotent. And we found men who claimed to have goodwill because they could also claim impotence. But with both kinds we saw the need to confront institutions rather than individuals. This is not to deny the value of individual cooperation but simply to say that in this nation change cannot be made through individuals. The structures of the nation respond only to amassed power, not to verbal or moral appeals. Thus we saw that in order to effect change we would have to create coalitions of power as massive as the institutions we opposed.

History might have taught us this lesson if we had listened. Historians of social change have often pointed out that no society willingly surrenders any part of its own power except when it is in its own interest. But this was something we came to learn through our own struggle and failure.

America would not give us our rights just because we pointed out that it was the correct thing to do. Rights, after all, are potential power. We were looking at justice and equality before the law as moral, ethical, and human questions. Those we faced saw more accurately that these were the coordinates of eventual power. If equal rights were granted to Black people, they would be able to participate equally in all areas of the national life, and the old roles of master and slave would be discarded forever. This was too high a price for America to pay for a mere moral principle.

Rather than surrender to the righteousness of the Black cause, white America preferred to spend a little on token concessions to Blacks. To that end, a pattern of charity was developed. Select Black leaders were isolated and elevated, and concessions were channeled through them; in return they were to be responsible for keeping peace. This created the illusion of integration without ever threatening the real sources of control.

In this way, the white majority was able to purchase its measure of peace and get in the bargain pawns for the interest game of its power blocs. What we had to learn was that when white America gave, it was for *its* good, not for ours. We had to learn that charity is not love, certainly not the kind of love we saw as being essential to a humane society. We therefore had to learn to deal with white America on its own real terms, the terms of power.

It was at this point in history that the cry "Black Power" began to drown out the sweet strains of "We Shall Overcome." And the hysterical response which that cry received from the heart of the nation was characteristic. For what did America really have to fear from Black Power? The thing which even we saw only vaguely then was that this cry marked the turning point in our movement, from protest to politics, American style. Yet anyone who was really afraid of the simple Black demands which were being made must have been afraid because they thought it would be necessary to fight to the death against them.

Most Americans did not even ask themselves what Black Power might mean or how it might be translated into practical, political terms. They merely reacted with fear and rage. They did not care what it meant or represented. They were unable to comprehend it when it was explained. Their immediate response was so violent that it effectively prevented understanding.

Judging from the white reaction, one would have had to assume that America was 90 per cent Black rather than 90 per cent white. One would have had to assume that Blacks were on the verge of swarming over the white heartlands of the nation in an orgy of slaughter, pillage, and rape. One would have had to assume that an impoverished and distressed tenth of the nation, without tools or technology, without resources or weaponry, was about to overwhelm the forces of the most enormous and sophisticated military machine ever assembled. One would have had to assume that these two simple words, *Black Power,* signaled the sure collapse of Western civilization. And many whites apparently did assume all this.

But, in fact, the cry which so terrified the white majority seldom had any reference to whites at all. It was most often used as a rallying slogan for Black unity. When finally it was extrapolated into a practical political program by Stokely Carmichael and Charles Hamilton in their book *Black Power,* it could be seen as an inoffensive project of economic betterment which would clearly profit the entire nation, white perhaps even more than Black.

Why then does the cry still strike such fear? It seems to open a Pandora's box of insecurities which America deposits in the heart of each white citizen. It looses nameless fears, unattached terrors, free-floating feelings of dread, and focuses them all, quite irrationally, on Black skin.

Most whites cannot and will not understand Black Power because they cannot and will not understand Blacks, the position Blacks have in American society, or the function Blacks have in the American mind. Most whites cannot yet understand the simple fact that Blacks are human beings who want nothing more dangerous than to be treated as such, who have a very human aversion to being used as property, a very human inclination to resist such treatment, and an equally human impatience, after four hundred years, with those who are perpetuating their human destruction.

12

At the Bottom of the Melting Pot

Another of our assumptions was that we were dealing with an open society. We believed what we had been taught—that America was the great melting pot, that this was a society to which any group or individual could contribute, and, in return, be able to fully participate in the national life. We assumed that this was the way America worked and that, for special reasons, Blacks had simply been unable to take part in this process.

We soon learned, however, that despite the Fourth of July rhetoric, America is not one big happy family composed of many ethnic groups with only the Blacks excluded. America is in fact a collection of lonely ethnic islands, and other exclusive divisions; the seeming unity as a nation is really the precarious balance of power through which each body protects its own hard-won privileges. We learned that no one in this culture has any status apart from the power base from which he operates. And we learned that no one of *any* color who happens to be poor and unorganized has any civil rights which other people need respect.

In the South, where we began, this disunity was not so apparent to us. There, ethnic identity is more or less homogeneous; and there, the contrast between Black and white overrides every other tie or alignment. But when The Movement came to the Northern cities we met the hard reality of brute American pluralism.

In the Chicago neighborhood of Gage Park we protested de facto segregation and were the targets of more viciousness and filth than any place we had ever been, including the Deep South. Nuns and priests who marched with us were spit on and vilified by the Catholic residents who gathered in enormous numbers to howl obscenities and stone us. Almost every window in a business district we marched through was broken by the mobs who surrounded us. Every march was punctuated by bottles bursting into blood against the marchers' heads.

A great many of those who attacked us were obviously immigrants. They screamed at us in heavy accents, "Go back where you came from," or, "Go back where you belong"—wherever those places might be. It would have done no good for us to point out that we had been here in America for four hundred years. Even if they were just off the boat they had already learned the rules. They knew the nation was theirs because they were white; and they believed that they could never share it with us, because we were Black. Neither citizenship, nor length of residence, nor patriotism, nor dedication could make Black men Americans in their eyes.

After one march, two priests from the area and several laymen joined some of us to discuss what had happened. One of the priests said that he had known there were problems but that he had not had any idea the problems were so bad. A layman smiled and said, "We knew it,

Father." This man went on to explain that everyone in the area hated each other—Poles hated Letts, Serbs hated Italians, Germans hated Irish. And the priest responded by saying, "Yes, it's true. I still think of myself as an *Irish* Catholic priest, not just as a Catholic priest."

What happened in Gage Park was that all the hatred whites had for each other was redirected when Blacks showed up. For once, every nationality could join together in a common project—hating Blacks. When the Blacks left, the whites went back to hating each other again. This kind of thing happened so often in the North that we learned to stop listening to what the politicians told us about brotherhood just before election time each year. We had found out what they told each other in those smoke-filled back rooms. There, the question was posed without rhetorical dress. And the question was simple: how to get the Irish vote, how to get the Jewish vote, how to get the Italian vote.

Nigger is not the only term of ethnic slander which the nation has produced. Every group has been given its own: *wop, hunky, lugen, frog, kraut, greaser, kike, gook, chink, spic, cracker, peckerwood, hillbilly.* Every big city has not only its Chinatown, but neighborhoods where Lithuanian or Swedish is still the dominant tongue. And the interpersonal tension, the plain hatred, where these neighborhoods meet each other is scarcely less than where Blacks meet whites.

Each of the great immigrant groups to arrive in America faced some kind of discrimination on the part of those who had arrived earlier and had come to consider themselves natives. In fact, the term *native* could not be legitimately applied to anyone but the American Indians. Yet millions upon millions came and were Americanized, came and were accepted.

Blacks, of course, were here all the time. We watched each of these groups arrive and make good. And we retained our faith in the nation, believing that one day we would find our place just as each of these other groups had found theirs.

One thing we did not understand was that the others had *fought* for what they got. Our history books had never told us about the Irish riots in New York and Boston, or about the Germans marching on the Chicago city hall with guns. We thought these people had made their way by hard work and cunning thrift alone. We did not know that these immigrant groups had *organized* to achieve the power they commanded. They did not work in isolation, they worked together. They organized political clubs and used the power of bloc voting. They took over labor unions and kept the membership exclusive. They created their own banks for their own use. They built up businesses and brought their own people into them. They took care of their own.

Yet we heard over and over again, especially from second and third generation immigrants, how their parents came to America in poverty, how they struggled against enormous odds, how they finally won their way through striving and saving. And we never doubted the truth of this, though we knew that we had never been permitted even to enter this struggle.

So we were challenged to emulate the immigrant model, to pull ourselves up by our own bootstraps. And we tried; we tried in every way we could find. Consider the pathetic attempts made by Blacks to integrate the United States Army. We wanted to be a part of this nation in any way we could. We even begged to be allowed to fight white America's wars. And when manpower became scarce enough, we were allowed to enlist as cooks and kitchen help. When manpower became critical, Blacks were put on the front lines.

The same circumstances have held in the area of employment. It is true that newspapers once carried advertisements for employment with notes such as, "No Irish Need Apply." But that is a far cry from the quality of discrimination which Blacks still face today.

Not long ago, a Black boy in Chicago went into a white neighborhood looking for a job and was beaten to death by a gang of kids with baseball bats. How many Irishmen have been lynched for trying to find work? How many Poles have been hung from trees, had their genitals cut off and sewn into their mouths with wire, and then been roasted to a slow death because they failed to say "Mister"?

Many immigrant groups have faced language barriers, resentment, active hostility, and even violence. But the only other group in the nation's history to face this kind of systematic hatred was the one which originally owned the land—the American Indians—the group which the immigrants slaughtered.

There have been other groups who faced color barriers too, and their experience is instructive. There were Orientals who endured disgusting brutality and humiliation. But they never came in very large numbers. And they brought and retained a tightly knit culture with engrained habits of husbandry and hard work: Once they were released from the railroad gangs they were scarcely seen outside their restaurants and laundries. And they have certainly not assimilated; they have merely formed enclaves. Color seems to be the final barrier in America.

Finally, there are the Puerto Ricans, Mexicans, and other Latin Americans who have arrived. These people seldom find themselves any better off than the Blacks. They too are forced to live in ghettos and to labor at the most menial jobs. They too meet with discrimination at every step they take in America.

There were other factors involved in the failure of Blacks to succeed in the same way that the early immigrants did. Free Blacks in the North had gained a small measure of economic advantage even before the Civil War; but what little they had was actually taken by the immigrant groups such as the Irish who began pouring into the United States in the 1840s, escaping from the potato famine in their homeland. In the economic struggle which accompanied this influx, many jobs which had formerly been filled by Blacks—barbering, for example—were taken over by whites.

But the bulk of the Black population at that time was concentrated in the rural South. As late as 1900, nine out of every ten Blacks in the country lived on Southern farms. By the time these people started moving North, industrial opportunity was greatly diminished. The largest migration took place during the boom of the Roaring Twenties; and the majority of these Blacks arrived just in time for the Great Depression. Not until ten years later did employment open up substantially again.

Another basic difference between Blacks and the immigrant population was that the immigrants were always considered to be *eventually* assimilable, while Blacks still are not. Yet projections indicate that during the next two decades most of the major cities in the United States will gain Black majorities. This approaching change has led to a certain acceptance of some forms of integration by certain far-seeing individuals whose power is at stake. A recent plan to desegregate the Chicago schools, for example, openly states that its purpose is to prevent Chicago from becoming a Black city, not to improve the quality of education. Thus we see *integration* being used in an attempt to prevent Blacks from gaining the political power which might begin to alleviate their condition.

It is also fair to point out one final difference between the Blacks and the immigrants. This is the fact that most immigrants came to America because they knew opportunities were open for them here. Even when they were escaping from disaster in their homelands, they *wanted* to escape *to* America for good reason. Blacks, on the other hand, were captured and carted here as chattel. America never meant for them to have any other place. So Blacks have found the double cruelty of being refused admission to the society, and then of having the effects of this discrimination held up against them as proof of their inferiority, lack of capacity and general inability.

So we learned how little the melting pot has really melted, even with whites. Early in The Movement we did not see this. We did not understand how deeply divided the country was. We did not guess that the nation could contain so much hate, hate for itself, whites hating whites. But once we understood this, we came to see how futile it was to expect white America to permit the assimilation of Blacks. Then we began to take up the same strategies which other groups had used. We began to organize, for protection, for progress, and for power.

13

Democracy in America

Our next assumption was created in the same way as all the others. We believed what America said about its politics. We believed that democracy was the soul of the nation. We assumed that if we showed enough concern for that democracy we would be rewarded with participation in it. For, one hundred years after the passage of the Fifteenth Amendment, most Blacks were still, by one means or another, disenfranchised.

In the South there was the kind of disenfranchisement perpetuated by arrogant registrars backed by white mobs. A Black man might have to recite the entire state constitution from memory, comma for comma, in order to prove his literacy. A white man before the same registrar might prove *his* literacy by having someone witness his "X."

Restrictions such as this would have been comic had there not been so much at stake. But we accepted them because we had to; and we began voter registration drives. Yet, after memorizing the constitution down to its final punctuation mark and reciting it in the prescribed manner, Blacks often found they had won the privilege of voting at the expense of their right to live. They were fired from their jobs, welfare payments were cut off, mortgages were foreclosed, churches were bombed, and children were murdered. The entire bar-baric catalogue of Southern justice was enacted.

Yet we persisted, for one thing was clear to us—the thing Malcolm X summed up in the phrase "The ballot or the bullet." It was clear that Black people had to become effective in the control of their own lives. Only the means to this control were in question.

As we turned North, however, we found another kind of disenfranchisement, a more subtle form of discrimina-tion, practiced by the less blatant Northern politicians. Here, Blacks were not only allowed but actually en-couraged to register and vote, under the tutelage of The Machine.

The Machine survived by means of patronage, which allowed thousands of Black women to work at menial jobs such as cleaning the city's halls and hospitals, libraries and schools. It allowed them to scrub as long as they voted for the right party and returned a tithe of their pitiful wage to the party treasury. Black men faced the same exploitation. They were allowed to clean outside, in the parks and on the beaches, in the streets and in the alleys, for less than a living wage, which was further decimated by enforced donations to the party's "flower fund."

Those for whom such jobs could not be found were put on welfare, and continuation of that welfare was made contingent upon proper voting. Precinct captains made it clear that every welfare mother had to do her part in order to protect herself. This came not only as a threat but as a promise—a promise of added welfare payments, jobs, or better housing, *if* the precinct delivered enough votes to be eligible for its privileges.

Thus, the control of a precinct usually required no heavy-handed tactics. If the precinct captain knew his job, he didn't have to follow anyone into the voting booth. He knew how many were registered and who they were. He knew how many were Democrats and who voted. Beyond that, some simple mathematics and a little understanding of human nature was all he needed to figure out who voted how. Once that was known, proper pressure could be applied.

This was the system which also produced the Black machine politician—who for all practical purposes was a painted white man. This man was referred to on the street as "the nigger with the hole in his head"—a richly expressive folk symbol. The "hole in his head" was first of all a wound which destroyed this man; but it was more than that. It was a lens through which city hall and the Black community viewed each other, a telescopic lens. When the Black community looked through *its* end of the telescope at city hall, everything looked very, very big. But when city hall looked through the other end at the Black community, everything looked very, very small. It was the function of the "nigger with the hole in his head" to perpetuate the colloquy between the two on these terms.

If by chance a Black man showed up without a hole in his head, there were other ways of dealing with him. He was isolated. His constituents were removed from the patronage rolls. Services in his area were cut off. His name disappeared from the ballot. His petitions were disqualified. He was gerrymandered. His district was destroyed by highway and urban renewal projects. Or he was simply denied his seat, as was the case with Julian Bond and Adam Clayton Powell.

Yet this form of disenfranchisement functioned in poor white communities as well. Because of this our movement gained a new focus in the North. Integration became more than a demand by Blacks to get "in" to white society. Rather, it became the key concept around which Blacks and whites worked together to build a new society, to revitalize the democratic process. As Dr. King often said, "This is a Movement to save the soul of America, not just Black people, but Black and white together."

Yet whether they are Black or white, the ability to cast a vote every four years to help determine which millionaire will misrepresent them does not bring poor people flocking to the polls. Since their votes are ineffective, their real political power is not increased by voting, and consequently their motivation to continue voting is lowered still further. It is still another vicious circle.

We in The Movement maintained a rock bottom concern for democracy, trying to break out of that circle. We maintained a concern that civil liberties would become more than just words on paper, a concern that the Bill of Rights be truly implemented as the basic document of American freedom.

We were dealing with the central cleavages of American society in a way which we hoped would allow a concerned nation to solve its fundamental problems and deal with its social imperatives in order to keep itself from becoming totally divided. We assumed that this was, in fact, the American program. We assumed that if we showed enough concern for democracy, democracy itself would be renewed and show concern for us.

But the response we got was far too small to make for change. We began to see that the very idea of democracy had been stillborn in America. Blacks, for example, were never included. Democracy, like justice, was a privilege rather than a right. The Constitution never guaranteed anyone the right to vote. Even the specific voting rights amendments simply state that certain reasons, such as sex or a previous condition of servitude, shall not be used to deny suffrage.

Precise qualifications for voting have always been left up to the states. And most states initially adopted a variety of qualifications and restrictions, notably those which limited voting to landholders. Pitched battles were often required to see these qualifications changed so that laborers, mechanics, and other landless citizens could gain some measure of control over their government. Later, women fought to have the privilege extended to them. In general, the voting booth has been jealously guarded and finally opened only to those groups who have been willing to take to the streets to fight for suffrage.

Participation in the political life of the nation has never been granted fully or equally on the basis of the innate worth of individual human beings. In fact, nothing seems harder for most Americans to grasp than the idea that all men are somehow created equal. Democracy in this sense has never fully penetrated the

American conscience. And, in fact, a nation which was largely built upon the institution of holding human beings as property could not be expected to come to this concept readily.

In the light of this background, it is not surprising that white America's concern for democracy is even less potent today than when the nation was born. Two hundred years of practicing what is preached against have sapped the American doctrine of its force. White America for the most part does not even seek democracy for itself.

An obvious demonstration of this was the nation's easy acceptance of the 1968 Democratic convention. Eighty per cent of the Democratic voters who turned out in the primaries cast their ballots for peace candidates. One of these was shot down before the convention began. The other was simply ignored by the party professionals who gathered at Chicago to violate the will of the people.

More subtle instances abound—over half a million Americans are fighting a war which Congress never declared; there is a fatalistic public acceptance of political collusion with organized crime; there are endlessly repeated examples of price-fixing and consumer fraud which are simply ignored; political candidates are packaged and peddled by advertising firms just like detergent; most of the information necessary to intelligent citizen participation in national affairs is kept secret— what is released is a pack of lies politely referred to as a "gap" in credibility.

A genuine, functioning democracy would not operate in this way. It would require many of the same inputs necessary to any vital people's movement. It would require the consent and regular participation of its members, supported by free access to information and open discussion. It would require lines of mutual responsibility and accountability between the representatives and the represented. It would require an ability for the body politic to design and obtain laws which served it and promoted its ends.

The typical American seems to have stopped fighting for these things, or even thinking about them. His level of protest may rise as high as cynicism about the CIA or griping about the IRS. But in general he views his manipulation without any sense of moral outrage. He accepts the elite's view of him as a working IBM number waiting to be mined. He has rejected his own human worth.

So, if individual Americans have lost the dream of personal freedom, if they have accepted as overlords the vast, interlocking systems of business, education, politics, and the military which make their choices for them, then that abdication is reflected in the average man's experience with democracy. We found that we could not bring people who have given up democratic ideals for themselves into a struggle for *our* democratic rights.

This was the source of much of the confusion about what we in The Movement wanted. Many people simply could not believe that we were fighting over simple issues such as the right to vote. To them, that right did not seem worth fighting over; so they saw plots and conspiracies behind what we were doing, or they simply lapsed into headshaking confusion over what we were up to.

The Movement discovered that democracy, for all practical purposes, is not the working ideology of America. Dozens of our people lost their lives through lynchings, bombings, and murders, trying to put federal laws into effect in situations which the government was unwilling to face. When The Movement put democracy to the test, the democratic facade was quickly dropped to reveal the naked power with which the entrenched potentates guard their privilege. The real beliefs of the society were exposed beneath the superficial democratic exterior.

Nonviolence managed to provoke a series of confrontations with the Bull Connors of the North and South. These confrontations forced the government to pass civil rights legislation. But the test of legislation comes with enforcement; and for the most part the government has left enforcement up to those who are most opposed to it. We have, for example, just seen the director of the government bureau which is supposed to guarantee equal employment opportunities fired from his job for trying to enforce the law under which the bureau operates.

What we had perceived as a concern for democracy in this nation was merely a narcotic smoke screen designed to prevent us from seeing the reality beyond. We dealt with this smoke as if it were actual fact, and we were truly seen by our oppressors as rhetorical and inconsequential. We failed, but we learned.

In that ten-year test of American politics, we learned that democracy, if it is to live here, will have to be introduced anew by emerging peoples who still retain the ideals and are willing to fight to achieve and maintain them. America in general has decided that it cannot fight city hall. But we in The Movement have decided that we must. We have decided that we cannot rest until each man can take part in determining his own destiny, until this level of suffrage is extended to all, not as a privilege but as a right.

Our tactics are now directed toward acquiring the power necessary to make our voices heard and answered. Our strategy is directed toward reshaping the institutions of the nation so that this kind of power is unnecessary, so that *individuals* have power, no matter what their class or color, so that democracy can function.

14

Christian Love and Christian Hate

We also assumed that we were living in a nation that was rich in Christian love. Christianity was so basic to our movement, and seemed so fundamental to the life of the entire nation, that we made the assumption that our success would come through Christian action and Christian organization, by means of Christian love. We assumed that if we loved actively and courageously, if we showed love not only for our people but for our nation and its principles, then love would be returned. This belief was central to the morality of nonviolence.

The assumption of effective love stemmed directly from our basic faith in the principles of Christianity and our deep belief in America as a Christian nation. It was not that we were blind to the hatred which surrounded us but that we believed that hatred could be changed. We believed that Christianity was more basic to the fiber of American society than bigotry.

So we made love the basis of our appeal, the basis of our assault on abusive power and injustice. Love was at the bottom of our faith in nonviolence and our belief that this nation would respond to nonviolence with deliverance. Every nonviolent demonstration is in fact a complex act of love, an offering of brotherhood, an appeal to basic human motives, and a statement of the human condition. We believed that the cause of our condition was misunderstanding; and we believed that love could conquer misunderstanding.

Thus we moved into the streets, with our hands empty and our hearts full. But we found that this was not, was never, enough. It was enough to force the creation of a few congressional acts, but it was not enough to bring about national action. It was enough to bring thousands of individuals into our movement, but it was not enough to move the nation.

Yet it was natural, inevitable really, that we should have begun in this way. Black people are religious people. For many, the church is their life. It was impossible for us to believe that churchgoing whites could worship, hear sermons, read the Word of God, study the Gospels, sing hymns, accept Christianity, and open themselves in prayer without opening themselves to the love of other men.

We looked at the huge white Baptist, Methodist, Lutheran, and Presbyterian churches and felt that they must hold allies, that they could be brought into our cause if only our faith could make them respond. The Southern Baptist Convention alone has over eight million members, towering buildings, vast educational plants, multistaffs, enormous budgets, wealth, and social influence. It was impossible for us to believe that such an institution could be committed to exclusion, privilege, reaction, and racial hatred. Yet that is how the Southern Baptist Convention was born, and that is how it lives.

We felt that if we raised the issues openly, if we conveyed the truth in simple humility, the church and its members would respond with loving and creative human effort. But our attempts merely to integrate the churches were met with such viciousness that we were forced to change our minds. Individual churchmen joined us, but the institutional church remained an inflexible bastion of the status quo.

In the South, the white church became an even more resolute and forceful enemy of change. While Black churches were burned and bombed, white citizens' councils had the backing of their own churches. It is no accident that the rhetoric of the Ku Klux Klan is steeped in Christian piety. Christianity for the Klan and many other churchgoing whites consists largely of hating Blacks.

The white church has historically been a patron of the slavemasters and that heritage persists today. The white church has developed in such a way as to give its members assurance of their rectitude without reference to their actions. It has functioned to assure them that God was on their side, even when they were performing the most hideous and savage deeds. It has, whether intentionally or not, filled them with self-indulgent and self-righteous bigotry.

After ten years of our struggle, a study was made which notified the nation of something we had already learned in more penetrating ways. The fact is that white churchgoers are substantially more bigoted than individuals without religious affiliation. The churches are havens of intolerance.

Another study, a five-year sociological analysis of this problem, has shown that the vast majority of white

Framing Arguement of Movement

churchgoers admit that they are bitterly opposed to Black aspirations and have contempt for church leaders who support The Movement. They feel that the church should stay safely in the spiritual realm of individual inspiration and not meddle in social issues. They do not even want brotherhood preached, much less practiced.

Our early experiences in The Movement made it difficult for us to see these things. At Selma, for example, there was an abundance of the kind of Christian love we counted on, but it was less than it seemed. While it was all collected in a single small town in a backward state, it seemed invincible. Once it was spread across the nation, however, it dissolved in the institutional and individual pride and prejudice that is so much of the national life. It was all but lost.

The marchers at Selma formed a vanguard phalanx of Christian witness. But they were too few to turn the American tide. Even among those who joined our movement, too many did so in word alone; too many spoke, yet failed to act; too many prayed, but did not protest; too many called for reason, but kept themselves far from the fields where reason battled with brute force.

We found that we could not call up enough love in enough hearts to change the course of the nation. Love is very specific and personal. Love is based on an acceptance of human worth, a recognition of human dignity, a concern for human rights. What favorable response we did get from the nation was general and impersonal, based on completely different values. It came in the form of legislation concerning interstate commerce and public accommodations. It said, "You are interstate commerce, so you don't have to sit in the back of the bus." It did not say, "You are human beings and therefore must be free of inhuman indignities."

Eventually we began to suspect that the nation had neither the legislative vocabulary nor the Christian determination to deal with the issues we were raising. The issues had, finally, very little to do with a cup of coffee or a seat on a bus. They had to do with a Christian conception of inviolable human worth.

Consider the case of a Southern sheriff, who, along with several of his townspeople, is tried in federal court for violating the civil rights of three young Movement workers. This sounds like petty crime; and the defendants are indeed given light sentences. Yet, in fact, they interfered with the civil rights of these three young men by murdering them, with malice, premeditation, and torture. A jury of their peers in the local court had already acquitted them of the murder charge.

Both the vocabulary and the procedure of this case are instructive. Together they explain how far law is from being a tool of justice—as far as the American church is from being an instrument of Christian love. The humane values of Christianity are nowhere to be found in American legislative, judicial, or church actions.

If the values of this nation can be judged by its acts, then America has demonstrated that it can measure money but has no gauge for the quality of human life. This is a nation in which property, production, and profit receive the fullest measure of protection under law; but it is also a nation in which life and liberty are privileges, not rights. This is a nation in which the privileged maintain their pride by comparing themselves with those they have impoverished, imprisoned, and maimed. This is a nation that understands dollars but is blind to human dignity.

Yet as the nation heard and rejected our appeal it rejected its own finest teachers as well—all, including Christ, whose first sermon was against racial intolerance. It demonstrated beyond the shadow of a doubt that it was incapable of acting on the finest understandings of Western civilization. And it showed, finally, that it never fathomed the motives of our protest. So we could no longer assume that this was a nation which operated on Christian love. And we could no longer base our strategy on the assumption that Christian love was basic to the nation's life. America was unable to respond to love; and we were unable to succeed with loving appeal.

15

Man and Machine

We further assumed that America *had* the answers which would alleviate our situation. We knew that the nation had systematically placed us where we were. And we believed that it could equally well put us where we wanted to be. We felt that this would simply be a matter of demonstrating the reality of our problems and convincing the nation of the validity of our demands. It seemed to us that the skill, the understanding, the power, and the total capacity to solve our problems existed within the resources of the nation.

It was impossible for us to believe that a culture as powerful and inventive as the United States, with its massive investments in science and technology, with its apparent benevolence, could not, or would not, solve its domestic problems if it was once forced to face them.

It was impossible for us to believe that this country would not be eager to deal with the justice and humanity of our cause once it recognized them. But we found that this too was a mistake. We found that America is without the spiritual, moral, or intellectual resources necessary for dealing with its human and social problems. This nation does not have the answers because it has never sought them. It has used its skills on one kind of problem only. It has applied its technology to economic questions, but never to human ones. It has never even given human problems full problem status, and it is so thoroughly materialistic that it may not be able to.

Two centuries of dealing on a purely materialistic value system, two centuries of avoiding all of the most pressing questions of civil liberties and the rights of man, two centuries of refusing to deal with the question of human dignity, have robbed the American social structure of the sensitivity and understanding necessary to innovate social changes for human ends.

Property in America is valued far more highly than people. Once we began, for example, to deal with the problems of slum housing, we found that the legislative and legal machinery provided admirable protection for the property rights of slum lords but offered no redress for the human rights of slum dwellers.

There was nothing to prevent a landlord from shutting off the heat, refusing to fix the roof, turning a deaf ear to the pleas of his tenants to make basic repairs in the walls, windows, and floors. There were no procedures for forcing landlords to destroy the hordes of insects which spread disease throughout their buildings, to remodel stairways which collapsed under children's feet, to use paint which would not poison infants, or to rid their buildings of the rats which attacked babies in their cribs. These things were regrettable, but permissible. To be sure, there usually were laws against them on the books. But they could not be enforced.

When tenants banded together and used rent money to repair the buildings themselves, they were immediately confronted with the swift, sharp edge of the American legal system. For this violated property rights. It was neither regrettable nor permissible. It was a crime. It brought sheriff's deputies sweeping in to cast these people onto the streets with their meager belongings.

Perhaps the most graphic and barbaric example of this American proclivity to worship property and disregard people was provided by the mayor of Chicago. He reprimanded his police force for leniency during the summer riots. He ordered his officers to "shoot to cripple or maim" anyone found looting, to "shoot to kill" anyone caught with a molotov cocktail. Yet neither of these crimes is legally punishable by death; and looting would, in most cases, not even classify as a felony.

Yet this mayor felt he was perfectly justified in ordering a policy of "shoot to kill." And in reaction to this pronouncement of official "shoot to kill," right-thinking Americans throughout the land applauded. They, too, believed that property was more sacred than humanity, that the destruction of woodwork and glassware was far more sinister than the destruction of human life.

But, of course, it also matters who steals what from whom. The executives of electronics firms may swindle the government of millions and receive only token or suspended sentences. Drug firms may bilk consumers of other millions and receive nothing more than toothless threats. But a Black man with a quart of gin is to be gunned down on the street. And this receives national acclaim because something is at last being done to stop crime.

So we learned that American ingenuity is inhumane and almost entirely mechanical. It could solve the most complex problems of production, could create the most sophisticated forms of machine technology, could devise the most elaborate systems of automation and cybernation. But it could not deal with a simple human problem such as hunger.

Former Treasury Secretary Joseph Barr estimates that fifty billion dollars a year are lost to the government through tax loopholes for the wealthy. Much of this is under the guise of keeping the economy functioning smoothly. At the same time, all of the welfare payments in the nation amounted to less than ten billion dollars in 1968. Eastland of Mississippi receives $42,000 a year as a Senator. In 1957 he received $157,930 in farm welfare payments for *not* planting cotton on his land. Yet he remains a strong foe of welfare for the poor.

When protests against such situations left the organized, nonviolent stage and broke out in spontaneous riot, gigantic sums began to be spent. But it was not on cures for hunger or poverty. It was on the machinery for repression. American ingenuity once more came forth with the only form of solution it knew how to devise— hardware, sophisticated antipersonnel weapons, chemical crowd control devices, the arms for riot suppression.

But how much ingenuity went into suppressing the *causes* for riots? What resources have been expended to redress the intolerable human conditions of which riots are only a symptom? The nation says it is trying. But what does this mean, even when it is serious?

A businessman sees that something must be done. He sees the squalid poverty, the racking unemployment, the festering human misery, the catastrophic deprivation. And he is a man of goodwill, a man who genuinely desires to help. So what does he do? Since he is a businessman, business is what he understands. He looks for a businesslike solution. He wants to get business involved in the reconstruction of the ghetto. He wants to bring the institutions of finance to bear on the problems of the inner city. He wants to see corporations interest themselves in alleviating the persistent deficiencies in education for the disadvantaged. And he constructs elaborate schemes for accomplishing these things, for getting business involved, on its own terms, that is, with a profit.

For the businessman, the whole question boils down to, How can you make a profit out of poverty? The problem is where the money will come from. Since, by definition, it cannot come from the poor, it must come from the government. But where will the money go? That question has already been answered, simply because of the way the original question was posed. It will go to the businessman, who has to make a profit. Otherwise, the whole thing doesn't work.

So, goodwill or not, this plan is a scheme to take tax money, much of which has come from the poor themselves, and give it to business as profit. There are, to be sure, more subtle and more enlightened versions of this scheme, but this is the basic outline. Many plans such as this have the capacity to accomplish substantial good for the poor. Yet they will never solve the problem because it is a human problem, and none of these plans has human motives or effects.

In human terms, when a man is hungry, the problem is how to get food to him, not how someone can make a profit on getting food to him—especially not in America where food surpluses are rotting in a thousand warehouses. But when we review the plans which businessmen have created to fight hunger, poverty, or unemployment, we see immediately that they are all based on the presupposition that someone must make a profit. This is the only kind of solution businessmen can come up with.

There are men in government who see the problems and want to help, many of whom have devised programs for aiding the poor in the most fantastically wealthy nation in history. These are political programs. Here politicians, not businessmen, profit.

With great fanfare and ringing speeches, highly paid administrators, who were lately party fund-raisers or campaign coordinators, begin their work. The funds which are allocated by Congress are doled out, down through functionaries who are put onto the payrolls at state, county, district, city, and division levels, decimated by executive expenses at every step, finally to arrive at the local office where precinct captains sit in smooth-worn chairs and direct the indigenous poor to private welfare agencies. This is called war on poverty. Some political programs, of course, are better. But they all work within this framework. All benefit politicians more than they benefit the poor.

To the businessman, solutions must come in terms of profit; to the politician, in terms of party expediency. But where are these human problems dealt with in human terms? Where are the hungry fed because they are hungry? Where do the poor receive because they are in poverty? America has no working human terminology. It functions within the vocabulary of economics, the ideology of production, and the ideal of consumption. It proceeds with the morality of the machine. Its accomplishments are mechanical. And its finest thinking is done by computers.

Having come to understand all this, we could no longer continue to believe that America had the answers to our condition. And it was, accordingly, impossible for us to go on acting as though these answers were available. We could see that we would have to devise answers for ourselves.

16

The People's Choice

We had assumed that America held the answers. But more than that, we assumed that America would implement those answers once we presented our case clearly to the nation. And again we were wrong. For we found not only that the answers did not exist, but further, that there was not even any concern about them. No one sought those answers, and no one would put them into effect once they were given.

We found that America did not want to deal with us or the issues we raised. It was bereft not only of answers but also of concern for those whose only power was the moral force of their suffering. We were confronting a society which had established its basic structures in such a way that it was inimical to humane response. It did not see such response as being required or even valuable. We were dealing with a society which counted costs in terms of affluence rather than in terms of the quality of life, a society which counted people in terms of production and consumption rather than in terms of human existence.

Once we saw that there were no answers available we began to develop them for ourselves. We produced plans for eliminating slums, for providing decent housing, for organizing and renewing neighborhoods, communities, and entire cities. But at each step we found ourselves facing someone who controlled property, power, or prestige, and who opposed us.

We were without property because we were poor. We could not fight the entrenched power because we were few and disorganized. We had no prestige because our demands ran counter to the entire trend of the society. The questions we were raising had no answers which the society could recognize. The condition we were in was said to be nonexistent in America; the wealthiest and most powerful nation in the world refused to see that millions of its people were poor and hungry, sickened by the battle against prejudice and the eternal striving against insurmountable odds. America still, after four hundred years, was blind to us.

But why? When anthropologists study a primitive culture and try to understand how it works, they are often baffled because the members of that culture give explanations which make no sense. If a member of the culture is asked why a certain ceremony is performed, he may say that the time has come, that the gods have willed it, that it has always been done, or that the crops will fail without it.

At this juncture, the anthropologist may decide that the ceremony is meaningless, or he may look further for answers. He may ask himself what function the ceremony has in this society. And he may, for example, decide that it is a ceremony which announces new relationships within the culture—as when a youth becomes of age and is ceremonially taken into manhood. But in order to do this he must go beyond the answers which his respondents within the culture give.

We can ask the same kind of question about the function of the Black population in American society. And we can easily see that it does no good to ask those who perpetuate the Black condition, for they will give reasons which make no sense. They may say that it is human nature, economic necessity, or simply the way things have always been. But if we investigate the function of this Black population, we can begin to see that in many ways—socially, psychologically, and politically—America needs the "nigger."

The Black man's slave role in America was determined by his economic function as the backbone of the plantation system. When that system was destroyed by emancipation it was swiftly re-created under another, and in many ways even harsher, set of rules.

Blacks became sharecroppers in a system of virtual peonage. Starting with nothing, they were forced to borrow to begin work. They borrowed seed, feed, tools, a mule, land, and food. And at the end of the year, after paying what was due for rent and "furnish," they were as often as not further in debt than when they started. If cotton prices were high, there might be a profit. In that case, the rent would go up and the price of "furnish" would be redoubled. This system continues today in some parts of the South. Its gradual extinction elsewhere was accomplished only by the collapse of the cotton market.

The Blacks who left the South during the twenties, thirties, and forties to seek industrial work in the North and Far West found themselves in a similar situation. When there was a high demand for labor, as during wartime, they were taken into the bottom of the industrial institutions, as clean-up boys, kitchen help, and common labor. But as soon as the labor situation eased, they were pushed back down and out. They were always the last to be hired and the first to be fired.

During periods of unemployment and labor struggles, they were used as strike breakers, which only seemed fair since they were usually restricted or heavily discriminated against by unions. Year in and year out, the Black population formed a reserve labor pool which could be called on in times of national emergency. In such times, this population was brought into the economy. The rest of the time it was merely policed.

Even today, detailed studies show that in an industrial metropolis like Chicago over three-quarters of the heavy manufacturers hire Blacks only for menial positions, if at all. In the larger industrial scheme, Blacks function as a market for the rejects of the economy—the rejected housing, used cars, second-hand clothes, and bad food.

Psychologically, the Black population fulfills the necessities of white supremacy. Many whites seem to operate on a level of insecurity so high that this alone sustains them. Many others use this as an excuse for not facing their true problems. Lynching, even if it is only verbal, quiets their frustration and makes the much more frightening and difficult task of rebellion against their true enemies unnecessary.

Socially, those in power use this psychological misfortune to keep the question of caste above the question of class. For if poor whites were to join Blacks in opposition to their common oppressors it would be not only the Southern power structure but also the political-industrial elite of Northern manufacturing cities that would be in deep trouble.

These poor whites, like all the poor and excluded in American society, are just a different kind of nigger as far as the rulers of the nation are concerned. In the South, especially, it is common to hear racial inferiority theories directed by upper-class whites against the "degenerate stock" of the "white trash."

So, after centuries of such relationships, America was incapable of seeing our problems as compelling, nor could it act realistically in relation to us. It did not see us for what we were, and it did not respond to the demonstration of human beings, because it had become a society whose primary values were based elsewhere.

A clear example of this tendency can be seen in the recent cries for "law and order." These have almost exclusively been demands made with reference to policing Blacks, not with reference to implementing laws guaranteeing human rights or to creating the kind of order in which civil rights could thrive. In fact, most of those who call for "law and order" specifically desire the abridgement of laws such as those based on the Bill of Rights.

We had learned that America is a nation that cares about the color of skin, but not about character. The ethics of the nation could not be extended to meet us because they had never included a universal notion of humanity. America had structured and internalized the patterns of paternalism so that it could no longer freely perceive Black people.

121

The same traits can be seen in American international relations. Foreign policy operates within the same system of values. America has set itself solidly against any progressive movements which would upset the current arrangements for channeling industrial raw materials and opening up new international markets. It does this no matter what the cost may be to the people whose nations are affected.

From all these things we learned not only that many of our assumptions were wrong, but also that it was useless to base tactics for freedom on the willingness of white society or its ability to reply. This taught us much about the nature of our oppression and something more about the spiritual poverty of white society. It also taught us much about what must be done to apply, or enforce, our solutions once we found them.

17

Conformity and Struggle

We made one final assumption which proved false, the assumption that a single ideology would serve to inform the movement for Black freedom and drive it to success.

Throughout the history of Black struggles for freedom in the United States, we have been tied at any one time to a dominant ideology, whether it was the appeasement policy of Booker T. Washington or the back-to-Africa movement of Marcus Garvey. Blacks have always sought *the* one way for the times, the single system on which to base their tactics, the one understanding of reality which would serve them as a foundation for movement. But during the last fifteen years we have learned that the obstacles to freedom are too great and the perceptions of Black identity too diverse for a single ideology to define the struggle.

Black people have suffered under multiple forms of oppression in highly varied situations. Thus, the forces against which they must act are many. Their conceptions and their responses are likewise varied. In action, we encountered our own diversity. At first this frightened and frustrated us. We tried to create a single-mindedness of purpose. Then slowly we began to realize that diversity could be the key to our strength if we could learn to work with an open acceptance of this diversity. We learned that diversity was not necessarily disunity.

With this understanding we realized that any ideology which has people behind it, any movement which has representative strength, is valid. We can no longer define the Black condition in an ideologically exclusive way. We must move with the people, to meet the struggle where it meets them. Only in this way can we realistically oppose the forces which oppress us.

One of the factors which makes this imperative is the nature of class within Black society. The effects of tokenism have functioned to atomize the Black population, have spawned clawing individualism at a time when solidarity and cooperation are most necessary. In addition to this, the Black population has formed itself into classes which reflect, like a cracked mirror, the dominant society. The Black professional class has received experiences different enough from those who are permanently unemployed to make cooperation between the two difficult.

Therefore, in order to gain the required cohesion, a pluralism of style and method must be accepted by all. Black professional people may fight for those forms of freedom which answer most specifically their needs, without undermining or questioning the validity of the demands made by other segments of the Black population. This is possible because there is a growing awareness that even though different parts of the Black population have different immediate needs the forces which oppose and oppress them are the same, and the solutions of that oppression are similar.

Considering the ways in which America is dealing with its Black population, we saw the need for a variety of approaches. Klan brutality cannot be attacked effectively in the same way as religious patronizing. Exclusion from trade unions cannot be successively broken down with the same tactics used to bring financial institutions to set more realistic guidelines for granting loans to Black businesses. Yet all these things must be dealt with; all are of crucial importance to the Black community.

Those of us who are nonviolent can no longer afford to reject calls for armed self-defense after our best leaders have been murdered. Those of us who are committed to political action can no longer afford to reject programs of Black capitalism. None of these programs can provide a total solution to the condition of Black people, but each one can help in some way. Reformers and revolutionaries can make common cause because both are moving in the same direction. Christians and Muslims can find common ground in the necessity to create new alternatives.

Anyone who starts to struggle at any place can go all the way to achieve the changes all desire. No single front is that much more important than another. What is right is what the people will work for, what they see, and what they believe. Any form of struggle which is both serious and effective must be accepted by all as legitimate.

Among ourselves we will deal with questions of what is *most* serious and *most* effective. Among ourselves we will explore the areas in which one group can cooperate with another, the tactics which demand coalition, the events which call for unified response. In this way we will open the channels of communication which will lead to amalgamated effort and coordinated activity.

But we can no longer allow ourselves to be split, allow our energies to be expended in internecine warfare, indulge ourselves in schismatic dogmatism which proclaims that success can only be gained in one way. Every movement is liable to this fault, so our best energies must be directed against it.

Part IV

PROLOGUE TO THE FUTURE

18

Failure and Reformulation

During the last fifteen years much has been gained in a few areas such as national legislation and a change of values within the Black community. Yet the goals we saw at the beginning remain largely unachieved. One measure of both our success and our failure is the cycle of rebellion and repression which has by now become common in almost every city. Our success is seen in the changed expectations of Black people. Our failure is defined by the unchanged list of horrors that describes the Black condition.

But today, in the minds of most people, the nonviolent movement as we once knew it is over. New strategies are emerging. New cries are being heard. In place of the old, fervent "Freedom Now" is the virulent chant of "Black Power," the cry of "All Power to the People." The most intense "activists" of The Movement are no longer singing of brotherhood on freedom rides through the South. They are coldly preparing underground networks and stockpiling arms and ammunition for urban guerilla warfare in the North. The number of spontaneous riots is dwindling, but the threat of planned violence is on the rise.

There is no way to fight this new mood—except with tanks and guns. There is no way to destroy this new

movement with tokenism or minor concessions. Thi
mood must be accepted and taken seriously by the whit
community, for it is already taken seriously by the Black

A revolution is in progress here. Only the *kind* o
revolution is in question. The time for choice has ar
rived. And it is not a choice that the Black communit
can make. The Black community can only respond t
the forces directed at it from the larger community. A
real change of style and content which takes Black need:
and Black demands seriously will increase the possibilities for peaceful coexistence. Continued repression wil
strengthen the forces of revolt.

White Americans must ask themselves what kind of
physical and psychological situation would make *them*
revolt. Only when they understand that will they understand what is taking place in the Black community.
People do not lightly take to the streets with their
grievances; it is an act of desperation. People do not
choose rebellion; it is forced upon them. Revolution is
always an act of self-defense.

Yet it is clear that a violent Black revolution will fail
quickly without allies. But it is not clear that there will
be no allies. If warfare breaks out, large sections of the
white community will join the Blacks; and by far the
largest section of the white community will do nothing
at all, no matter how they feel. Most of the brown
(Mexican and Puerto Rican) communities are already
committed to the struggle, simply because their situation is the same as that of the Blacks. And, in addition,
America's integrated army could not efficiently fight a
race war. Many troops have even refused summer riot
duty.

If war breaks out, it will begin with selective destruc-
ion of transportation and communication networks
which are crucial to the operation of the cities—commu-
er trains, telephone lines, and broadcasting facilities.
Effective crushing of this activity will require such massive retaliation that it will broaden a limited rebellion
into a community project.

If warfare breaks out, it will take much of America's
might to control it. But that force is now spread around
the world, pursuing America's overseas adventures in
Europe, Asia, and Latin America. What will happen in
these places if American forces are withdrawn? And
what help might come to the American rebels from
America's avowed enemies? What advantage might be
taken of a civil war in the land of the free?

Even if the revolution were to fail utterly, what would
be the price of putting it down? The price, as in the
case of the Indians, would plainly be genocide, the
destruction of a people. So, for those who are unwilling
to accept genocide as a national program, the time is
critical. A new kind of thinking must take place.

For those who are interested in seeking public alternatives to armed revolt, a new kind of seriousness is required. For those who are attempting to create programs that will in fact answer the needs of the time, a
new theory is necessary. We can no longer afford hopeful failures, halfway palliatives, or quarter-hearted programs that provide more for political hacks than for the
poor in whose name they are created.

Instead, America must ask itself seriously why people
are planning warfare. The answer is rather simple: we
have been driven to desperation by bondage to intoler-

able conditions. But what do we want? We want to determine the direction of our own lives and to be allowed to work to achieve our own goals. Anyone who wishes to think seriously must deal with these facts. America must prepare itself to release the slaves or to confront armed revolution.

It will no longer do to focus on the few exceptional Blacks who escape and enter the fringes of white society. It will no longer do to claim that America is a free country where anyone who really wants to get ahead can do so. That is a lie, and such a painful lie that Black people are no longer even willing to answer it. If that were true, Black people would *be* ahead and there would be no problem. But the Black condition is not due to lack of desire, ability, or striving.

Today, the Black communities are awaiting the final solution. The concentration camps are waiting. That much is known. And we have learned from our own experience, from the experience of the Indians, from America's conduct in Vietnam, that it *can* happen here. Hitler's reign of terror could be replayed on American soil with a new cast of characters.

We remember what happened during the Second World War. When the war started, a few Germans who were known agents of the Reich were arrested. Others who were suspected were investigated. As a whole, the German American population was simply ignored. But what happened to the nonwhite Japanese Americans? They were rounded up wholesale, citizens and aliens alike, and herded into concentration camps. Their homes and businesses were sold. Their property was

FAILURE AND REFORMULATION

onfiscated. They had no trials and no legal recourse.
What was taken was never returned. And white America
watched with scarcely a murmur as this atrocity was
performed.

Still, genocide is a strong word. It is hard to imagine
there could be an American will for it. Yet in the pages
of *Life* magazine we see a Black man gunned down in
the street for stealing a case of beer. A young boy is
blown open because he just happens to be standing
nearby. In Newark, national guardsmen open fire on
Black citizens who are simply looking out their windows.
In Chicago, a fourteen-year-old girl is murdered for
stopping in front of the broken window of a furniture
store. In Detroit, policemen and soldiers take Blacks
into a commandeered motel, torment, torture, and exe-
cute them. The list is endless. Anyone interested in draw-
ing up a list may consult the Kerner Commission Report.

White people, of course, find excuses or plead extenu-
ating circumstances for all of these incidents, or view
them, if they are forced to, as regrettable accidents. But
Black people no longer believe that their condition is
accidental. They see daily the slow genocide which has
long been taking place. They see entire communities
being destroyed by a systematic combination of starva-
tion, deprivation, and physical terror. They remember
the Jews in the Warsaw ghetto and they prepare to
defend themselves, to insure their survival.

Genocide is the overriding possibility against which
everything else must be judged. It has been government
policy before, with the red man. It has been tested with
the savage and unnecessary destruction of Dresden,

Hiroshima, Nagasaki, and much of Vietnam. These events belie the most fervid protestations of humanity. The nation has never shown any regret for these acts, any more than it has shown regret for its dehumanization of Black people.

Liberal sentiments mouthed in the halls of Congress on auspicious occasions are no proof against the daily violence toward the Black community. So the time for a final choice has come. The alternatives are clear, and those of us who still hope for a nonviolent end to this condition are growing fewer each day.

The time is gone when we can deal with anything but the most fundamental issues. The days of tokenism, accommodation, and co-option are gone. We must begin to engage the basic splits in our nation. And only to the extent that we deal realistically with these issues will we be able to meet the crisis of our times.

It has taken four hundred years to create this problem, and we do not expect it to be solved overnight. The thing we *do* expect is an effort which has a chance of solving it, of going all the way and doing the whole job.

Europe was almost totally wrecked by the Second World War. But America rebuilt it within a few years. The same type of commitment is required in building our own nation. Billions of dollars were spent to revive the war-ravaged nations, many of which we ourselves bombed to the ground. Yet we have not shown that kind of concern for our own land. A few years ago we might have said that we did not have the money. But we have the money to pour thirty billion dollars a year into Vietnam, a million and a half dollars a day, a thousand dolars a minute. We have that kind of money for destruction. Can we afford less for construction?

Money to answer America's needs can be found anytime a national will to answer those needs is established. In order to create that national will, we must have a new understanding. We must learn to think radically, to reach the root of the problem. We must learn to think radically about the causes of the Black condition, about the effects of that condition, and about a cure. We must do the hardest thing of all—we must heal ourselves.

We must think radically enough to begin reshaping this nation so that human values are supreme. We must begin to think about the question of survival, of survival for us all, and of how we want to survive. That is the most basic of all questions. *How do we want to live?* Today that question is being answered without being asked. Soon it will be too late to *choose;* an answer will be thrust upon us. And when we can no longer decide how we want to live, it will no longer be possible for us to live as full human beings. Right now, the day of our own judgment has arrived.